Praise for
The Missing Link to Help Them Think

Marilee Sprenger, the renowned "Brain Lady," has consistently delivered groundbreaking insights on the intersections of brain science, social-emotional learning, and effective teaching practices. In this book, Sprenger masterfully combines cutting-edge neuroscience with practical classroom strategies for nurturing both the minds and the hearts of students. Emphasizing the power of emotional connections for memory retention and engagement, *The Missing Link to Help Them Think* provides accessible, research-based techniques for creating inclusive, supportive, and dynamic learning environments. Whether you're looking to boost students' cognitive growth, enhance their emotional intelligence, or simply make learning more meaningful for today's classroom, this is the resource you've been waiting for!

—**Katie Garner**, author of *Secret Stories: Cracking the Reading Code with the Brain in Mind*

As an educator who has been teaching for more than 40 years on the neuroscience of play and the benefits of humor, I found *The Missing Link to Help Them Think* a must-read. Marilee Sprenger provides significant insights into the connection between executive function and social-emotional learning. She offers creative, playful strategies and hands-on activities for learners who cope with the challenges of underdeveloped executive function skills. The inclusion of self-assessment charts empowers both students and educators to be active participants in their learning journey.

—**Mary Kay Morrison**, author, educator, speaker, founder of *Humor Academy*, and director of Association for Applied and Therapeutic Humor

The Missing Link to Help Them Think is a great resource for anyone looking to merge social-emotional learning, brain science, and academic instruction. Marilee Sprenger has skillfully aligned the latest findings on brain research and SEL with clear, actionable teaching strategies for teachers. This indispensable guide recognizes that a child's cognitive and emotional development cannot be compartmentalized, and instead advocates for a holistic, integrated approach that acknowledges how children think and learn. For educators seeking to harmonize SEL with academic content, this book is the missing link you've been searching for. A must-read for anyone committed to nurturing the whole child and enhancing learning outcomes.

—**Lori Loving**, assistant regional superintendent, Regional Office of Education #33, Illinois

This exciting and insightful book explores executive function skills and social-emotional skills, the two biggest needs of your students today. Expect to get dozens of actionable, easy-to-implement tools that ensure your students soar!

—**Dr. Eric Jensen**, CEO of Jensen Learning

"Brain Lady" Marilee Sprenger has done it again! *The Missing Link to Help Them Think* puts the *learning* back into social-emotional learning. The co-learning aspect of transformative SEL explained in this book is critical to contemporary learning, where learning spaces are shared, effective, and respectful of every learner's needs, and promote belonging for all. This book is an overflowing toolbox of strategies for younger and older students alike. Whether you're working with children as a teacher or a parent, you need this book!

—**Mike Fisher**, ASCD author

The Missing Link to Help Them Think is the book teachers have been waiting for. Sprenger offers practical strategies that connect student behaviors with their executive functions and the social-emotional prerequisites that must be in place for learning to happen.

—**Cecilia Ryon**, NBCT, instructional coach, Deer Path Middle School, Lake Forest, IL

THE MISSING LINK to Help Them THINK

Also by Marilee Sprenger

101 Strategies to Make Academic Vocabulary Stick

The Essential 25: Teaching the Vocabulary That Makes or Breaks Student Understanding

Everyday Vocabulary Strategies
(Quick Reference Guide)

How to Teach So Students Remember, 2nd Edition

Social-Emotional Learning and the Brain: Strategies to Help Your Students Thrive

Vocab Rehab: How do I teach vocabulary effectively with limited time?
(ASCD Arias)

Marilee Sprenger

THE MISSING LINK to Help Them THINK

Connecting Executive Function and SEL Skills to Boost Student Achievement

Arlington, Virginia USA

2800 Shirlington Road, Suite 1001 • Arlington, VA 22206 USA
Phone: 800-933-2723 or 703-578-9600
Website: www.ascd.org • Email: member@ascd.org
Author guidelines: www.ascd.org/write

Richard Culatta, *Chief Executive Officer;* Anthony Rebora, *Chief Content Officer;* Genny Ostertag, *Managing Director, Book Acquisitions & Editing;* Susan Hills, *Senior Acquisitions Editor;* Mary Beth Nielsen, *Director, Book Editing;* Miriam Calderone, *Editor;* Lisa Hill, *Graphic Designer;* Circle Graphics, *Typesetter;* Kelly Marshall, *Production Manager;* Shajuan Martin, *E-Publishing Specialist;* Kathryn Oliver, *Creative Project Manager*

Copyright © 2025 ASCD. All rights reserved. It is illegal to reproduce copies of this work in print or electronic format (including reproductions displayed on a secure intranet or stored in a retrieval system or other electronic storage device from which copies can be made or displayed) without the prior written permission of the publisher. By purchasing only authorized electronic or print editions and not participating in or encouraging piracy of copyrighted materials, you support the rights of authors and publishers. Readers who wish to reproduce or republish excerpts of this work in print or electronic format may do so for a small fee by contacting the Copyright Clearance Center (CCC), 222 Rosewood Dr., Danvers, MA 01923, USA (phone: 978-750-8400; fax: 978-646-8600; web: www.copyright.com). To inquire about site licensing options or any other reuse, contact ASCD Permissions at www.ascd.org/permissions or permissions@ascd.org. For a list of vendors authorized to license ASCD ebooks to institutions, see www.ascd.org/epubs. Send translation inquiries to translations@ascd.org.

ASCD® is a registered trademark of Association for Supervision and Curriculum Development. All other trademarks contained in this book are the property of, and reserved by, their respective owners, and are used for editorial and informational purposes only. No such use should be construed to imply sponsorship or endorsement of the book by the respective owners.

All web links in this book are correct as of the publication date below but may have become inactive or otherwise modified since that time. If you notice a deactivated or changed link, please email books@ascd.org with the words "Link Update" in the subject line. In your message, please specify the web link, the book title, and the page number on which the link appears.

PAPERBACK ISBN: 978-1-4166-3324-2   ASCD product #124013   n11/24
PDF EBOOK ISBN: 978-1-4166-3325-9; see Books in Print for other formats.
Quantity discounts are available: email programteam@ascd.org or call 800-933-2723, ext. 5773, or 703-575-5773. For desk copies, go to www.ascd.org/deskcopy.

Library of Congress Cataloging-in-Publication Data
Names: Sprenger, Marilee, 1949- author.
Title: The missing link to help them think : connecting executive function and SEL skills to boost student achievement / Marilee Sprenger.
Other titles: Connecting executive function and social emotional learning skills to boost student achievement
Description: Arlington, VA : ASCD, [2025] | Includes bibliographical references and index.
Identifiers: LCCN 2024033627 (print) | LCCN 2024033628 (ebook) | ISBN 9781416633242 (paperback) | ISBN 9781416633259 (adobe pdf) | ISBN 9781416633266 (epub)
Subjects: LCSH: Affective education. | Executive functions (Neuropsychology)--Study and teaching. | Social learning.
Classification: LCC LB1072 .S683 2025 (print) | LCC LB1072 (ebook) | DDC 370.15/34--dc23/eng/20241009
LC record available at https://lccn.loc.gov/2024033627
LC ebook record available at https://lccn.loc.gov/2024033628

33 32 31 30 29 28 27 26 25   1 2 3 4 5 6 7 8 9 10 11 12

THE MISSING LINK to Help Them THINK

Acknowledgments ix

Introduction 1

1. Components of SEL and EFS 7

2. Impulse Inhibition 17

3. Working Memory 31

4. Attention and Focus 44

5. Cognitive Flexibility 56

6. Self-Monitoring 67

7. Planning, Organization, Prioritization,
   and Time Management 79

8. SEL and EFS: Fulfilling the Dream 88

Appendix A: Universal Executive Function Strategies 97

Appendix B: Modeling 104

References 110

Index 117

About the Author 123

Acknowledgments

There are so many people to thank! Thank you to the SEL researchers, authors, and presenters who led me to my first book on SEL and the brain and guided me through this book as well. Thanks as well to CASEL, which has a plethora of research and practical solutions and is always willing to listen and to change. Thank you to executive function gurus like Harvey Silver, Carol Searle, Adele Diamond, and Peg Dawson, who have taught me a lot. I want to thank Susan Hills, my acquisitions editor at ASCD, for her patience and willingness to help me home in on this project. Thanks also to ASCD copyeditor Miriam Calderone, who always makes me sound like a good writer, which is much appreciated. To my friends and family who had to listen to me constantly talk about this topic, thank you for remaining in my life. Of course, as always, thank you to Scott, my high school sweetheart, my best friend, and my loving husband, for putting up with my two careers for so long.

Introduction

Pop quiz: How many of the following student behaviors are you all too familiar with?

__Tardiness
__Forgetfulness
__Late homework
__Dawdling instead of starting a task
__Not knowing what to do when a task is finished
__Keeping a messy desk or locker
__Inability to work well with others
__Procrastination
__Inability to set or achieve goals
__Tendency to interrupt
__Inappropriate reactions to change
__Time blindness

Each of these challenges is due to underdeveloped executive function skills, or EFS. This book is about drawing a connection between what we already know helps kids attain positive behaviors and academic skills—social-emotional learning, or SEL—and the higher-level mental processes required to carry out tasks and reach goals: well-developed executive function skills.

Upheaval related to the COVID-19 pandemic has pushed many of us over the edge. The education system is still reeling, and there are more traumatized students and teachers than ever before. We are trying to catch up and keep up in a time of anxiety and turmoil. Schools are working hard to harness the power of social-emotional learning to ensure that all students learn in an environment that is welcoming, accepting, and safe. The Collaborative for Academic, Social, and Emotional Learning (CASEL) describes its SEL competencies as "an integral part of education and human development. SEL is the process through which all young people and adults acquire and apply the knowledge, skills, and attitudes to develop healthy identities, manage emotions and achieve personal and collective goals, feel and show empathy for others, establish and maintain supportive relationships, and make responsible and caring decisions" (CASEL, n.d.).

Despite the strides that have been and are being made to fulfill the dream of SEL, many students in SEL-enriched classrooms still have difficulty with academic content. Most likely, many of these students need help developing their EFS. While SEL prepares the brain and body to learn, EFS are necessary for learning to take place. These are the skills we use to remember, plan, and organize our lives. Executive functions control our working memory, mental flexibility, and emotional regulation (Kemna, 2022). The Center on the Developing Child at Harvard University (n.d.) describes these skills as "the mental processes that enable us to plan, focus attention, remember instructions, and juggle multiple tasks successfully. Just as an air traffic control system at a busy airport safely manages the arrivals and departures of many aircraft on multiple runways, the brain needs this skill set to filter distractions, prioritize tasks, set and achieve goals, and control impulses" (para. 1).

Executive function skills are not hardwired in the brain; we aren't born with them already in place. Though EFS can develop rapidly between the ages of 3 and 5, many students either have deficits or live in environments that prevent this from occurring. Development also tends to spike during adolescence and again in young adulthood. Between and during these stages, we can enhance our students' EFS by explicitly teaching those skills and providing opportunities to practice them.

Both EFS and SEL play critical roles in shaping cognitive, emotional, and behavioral aspects of a student's development; arise from the prefrontal cortex of the brain; and interact for student success. Executive functions control our ability to self-regulate and to initiate and complete tasks, and can be compromised by such factors as improper sleep, poor nutrition, excessive screen time, illness, and adverse childhood experiences—all of which can also affect social-emotional learning.

Just as SEL improves the emotional climate of your room, developing students' EFS will improve the academic climate. Helpfully, many SEL programs incorporate activities that explicitly target EFS, recognizing their interconnected nature and their impact on social, emotional, and academic success.

Experts in the relatively new field of traumatology tell us that early life relationships play an enormous role in the development of students' stress-response systems and their ability to form healthy relationships. When children experience early trauma, their brain development is arrested—to the point that a 5-year-old child might enter school with the brain development of a 2- or 3-year-old (Perry, 2023). The inability of such children to keep up with classmates causes further stress, exacerbating their difficulties.

There are many executive functions, but in this book, I am focusing on 10 (note that I group 4 together in the category of planning, prioritization, organization, and time management) that are discussed repeatedly in the literature on the topic. These functions emerge and develop gradually throughout childhood and adolescence (Guare et al., 2013).

1. **Impulse Inhibition**
   - Ability to inhibit responses to certain stimuli or control impulses
     – One of the earliest executive functions to develop; observed in infants with a toddler phase at around 18 months to 4 years
   - Ability to replace habitual or dominant emotional or behavioral responses with a more appropriate emotion or behavior to reach one's goals

2. **Working Memory**
   - Ability to hold and manipulate information for short periods
     – Begins to develop in the first 6 to 12 months of life; continues to develop throughout childhood and adolescence, often with a big spike between 3 and 5 years of age

continued

3. **Attention and Focus**
   - Ability to tune in and stay on task
     – Emerges in early childhood

4. **Cognitive Flexibility**
   - Ability to switch between different tasks or perspectives or think about multiple concepts simultaneously
     – Emerges in early childhood

5. **Self-Monitoring**
   - Ability to set and monitor goals
     – Becomes increasingly sophisticated in adolescence
   - Self-awareness and monitoring of thinking processes
     – Develops throughout childhood and usually blossoms in late adolescence

6. **Planning, Organization, Prioritization, and Time Management**
   - Ability to initiate tasks and plan actions
     – Emerges in middle childhood
   - Ability to organize, plan, prioritize, and manage time effectively
     – Develops in late childhood and adolescence

It's important to emphasize that EFS develop at different rates in different individuals and are influenced by both genetic and environmental factors. Moreover, different aspects of an executive function may develop at different rates within the same individual. Educational practices that encourage the development of EFS, such as providing opportunities for problem solving, promoting self-regulation, and incorporating activities that challenge cognitive flexibility, can support the maturation of these critical cognitive processes.

This book was written for every teacher, including those who work with neurodivergent students, and will also benefit parents and caregivers. It is my hope that the information presented here about executive functions helps you to better understand all your students, including those with autism or attention and behavior disorders. Many students are labeled according to the executive dysfunctions they present in the classroom. Once you and they have strategies to address those challenges, these labels may no longer apply to them. To further support your efforts, Appendix A offers universal executive function strategies that offer practice on many of the EF skills in this book. Because modeling executive function skills is the best way for educators to present these skills and the primary way students will attain them, Appendix B provides helpful modeling strategies.

Though educating every brain is a challenge, I hope this book helps demystify your students' struggles so you can help them flourish emotionally and academically both inside and outside the classroom.

Components of SEL and EFS

Humans aren't born with refined social-emotional or executive skills; rather, they develop these skills as they are modeled and taught to them and through life experiences. Though not innate, SEL skills and EFS are markers for success not only in school but throughout life. Before exploring ways to develop students' SEL skills and EFS in depth, it is important to examine the components of both.

The Three Domains of SEL

The results of a recent meta-analysis of 424 studies from 53 countries on K–12 SEL interventions show unequivocally that students who participated in universal school-based SEL interventions "experienced significantly improved skills, attitudes, behaviors, school climate and safety, peer relationships, school functioning, and academic achievement" (Cipriano et al., 2023). Unfortunately, too many educators ignore the academic side of social-emotional learning, focusing on the *social* and *emotional* and ignoring the *learning*.

At the beginning of the SEL movement, many schools integrated the concept into the classroom in the form of a weekly 30-minute session with an "SEL teacher" who came in to do activities with students. Although this approach isn't altogether useless, it doesn't fully meet the needs of students, either. Thirty minutes is not enough time for students to learn how to access their own emotions, label them, understand them, and control them. The best approaches to SEL are those that suit the learning context and that are crafted to support academic achievement.

Social-emotional learning consists of an emotional domain, a social domain, and an academic domain. Each of these domains plays a role in helping students better navigate the world of school. Stephanie Jones and her research team at the Harvard Graduate School of Education refer to these domains as "buckets" and as emotion, interpersonal, and cognitive regulation skills, respectively (Shafer, 2016). Whatever we choose to call them, the important point is to understand that these domains (or buckets) are categories of SEL competencies.

The Five SEL Competencies

The five SEL competencies presented here—self-awareness, self-management, social awareness, handling relationships, and responsible decision making—are based on the theories and work of several researchers, including Daniel Goleman's (1994) work on emotional intelligence. Emotional intelligence is the ability to identify and manage your emotions and the emotions of others, and SEL is the process by which children acquire emotional intelligence (Macmillan, 2020).

Self-Awareness

It goes without saying that if we are not aware of our own current feelings, it is almost impossible for us to deal with the feelings of others. Self-awareness—which involves recognizing one's emotions and thoughts and their impact on behavior—is the first step in accruing emotional intelligence. Students entering your classroom will be in one of the following three brain states, each of which affects their learning and behavior in different ways: the survival state, emotional state, and executive state. Self-awareness means knowing which state we are in at any given time.

The **survival state** involves our arousal system and our alarm system. The reticular activating system, located in the brain stem, is a network of neurons that filters out unimportant information and allows us to focus on what is important. For survival purposes, it will always focus on anything that is considered a threat. If threat is detected, it will send an alarm to various structures in the brain to protect us from the threat. The survival part of the brain is in charge of keeping us alive, so it checks out every possible threat. Although this state initially evolved to deal with life-or-death physical threats in the wild, it can also be triggered by all kinds of modern situations: feeling left out of a group, being deprived of possessions, getting cut off on the road, and so on. Once our inner alarm system goes off, our brains set different behaviors in motion—usually the fight, flight, or freeze response, depending on the circumstances. In the survival state, the brain is asking the question "Am I safe?" If the brain does not feel safe, it will remain in survival mode until things change. The survival state keeps us from entering higher levels in the brain where we can logically consider what is occurring and make rational decisions. In this lower survival state, learning doesn't occur.

The **emotional state** can be either positive or negative. When students come into the classroom happy and excited, it is easy for them to access the executive state, which is necessary for learning. The opposite is true if students come to class feeling sad or angry: If Alayna's mother yelled at her the entire way to school, you can imagine the state she will be in during class. The emotional state asks, "Am I loved?" For students in an emotional state to be able to learn, they must feel that they are now safe from any physical or verbal assaults. The emotional state is housed in the limbic system of the brain.

When in the **executive state**, the brain is relaxed yet alert. This is when you're in "the zone," able to get lots of things done. You know those days when you captivate your students and can see the aha moments on their faces? You're good, and you *know* you're good. There's nothing like the feeling of doing your job well, and it's the same for students, too. The executive state relies on the prefrontal cortex along with some subcortical structures. It asks the question "What can I learn?"

Self-Management

Once students know what state they are in, they can use strategies to manage the feelings that come with it. *Self-management* refers to the ability to regulate one's emotions, thoughts, and behaviors effectively in different situations. According to CASEL (n.d.), aspects of self-management include impulse control, stress management, self-discipline, self-motivation, goal setting, and organizational skills. (You may note that many of these are interrelated—for instance, self-discipline relies largely on impulse control—and include executive functions.)

Self-management often requires coping strategies aimed at calming the amygdala, the small almond-shaped structure in each hemisphere in the brain. When our stress response is dysregulated, the amygdala releases chemicals that create more stress in the brain and the body, such as cortisol, adrenaline, and noradrenaline, causing the prefrontal cortex that controls our emotions to basically shut down. Controlling the stress-response system requires us to coregulate alongside other individuals who are in a calmer state. The body always seeks homeostasis, or balance. If the stress-response system is working correctly, it will find that balance.

Students dealing with adverse childhood experiences may become so accustomed to a dysregulated stress-response system that it seems normal to them. They are desperately in need of a caring adult to help them coregulate. Positive experiences can help some students overcome the dysregulation caused by trauma, but they must have someone they trust to help them through the process. They also do best with predictability: patterned, repetitive, structured experiences in a trusting environment (Darling-Hammond et al., 2020).

Social Awareness

Our brains have developed to help us connect with others. We are social creatures who thrive on connections with our family, friends, and community. These connections are regulating as well as rewarding. When students grow up with family and neighbors who support them, their brains begin to predict how the world works; they start to believe that if everyone in their immediate world is kind and supportive, then others will be as well. By contrast, students who grow up in an environment bereft of support and kindness are conditioned not to expect those things and to be distrustful when they are offered. They have more difficulty with self- and social awareness. It may take these students longer to understand that the way they have been treated by some is not how all people will treat them. The ability to understand and manage one's own emotions is necessary to access areas of the brain that enable us to understand other people's emotions.

When students are aware of their emotions and can control them, they are able to examine and understand the emotions of others—a major step in relating to and interacting with others productively. Walking in someone else's shoes and respecting cultural differences play a big role in social awareness, which is essentially the ability to understand and empathize with others' emotions and perspectives. An emotional vocabulary is vital to the process of truly relating to others and communicating to them that you understand where they are coming from. Listening is also an important component of social awareness, and keen observation helps students to better understand other students and adults. These skills can all be taught to students who haven't had them modeled for them at home.

Relationship Skills

According to CASEL (n.d.), the following skills are necessary for establishing and maintaining healthy and rewarding relationships with diverse individuals and groups:

- Communicating clearly
- Listening closely
- Cooperating with others
- Resisting inappropriate social pressure
- Negotiating conflict constructively
- Seeking as well as offering help when needed

Because students closely monitor adult relationships at school, how you handle relationships with colleagues can heavily influence how they treat their classmates—and how they treat you. If you feel that relationships among your own peers need work, it may be advisable to engage in team-building exercises during staff meetings.

According to Rimm-Kaufman and Sandilos (2015), students who have good relationships with their teachers work harder for those teachers, are more likely to take academic risks, are more engaged, and are less likely to need disciplinary action than their peers. Positive teacher-student relationships have also been shown to increase prosocial behaviors like empathy, kindness, and gratitude (Beachboard, 2019).

To help students develop prosocial behaviors, consider having them keep gratitude journals where they can reflect on what they are grateful for. You can also have them write this information on entry or exit tickets or write them on sticky notes and display them on the wall. Some students can't imagine feeling gratitude, and seeing other students' reflections may encourage them to concentrate on the positive aspects of their lives.

Another strategy is to discuss random acts of kindness with students as they line up for lunch or before the bell, which can in turn give rise to such acts in the classroom. As students watch classmates being kinder, they are likely to follow suit. Keep in mind that some students don't see kindness modeled in their home environments, so it's especially important for them to see it in others. The same is true of empathy: As students see how you model empathy toward others (including fictional or historical characters), their empathy can grow.

Responsible Decision Making

CASEL (n.d.) defines *responsible decision making* as the ability to make constructive choices about personal behavior and social interactions based on ethical standards, safety concerns, and social norms. To those factors you might add cultural differences among students, the climate and culture of the school, and the many demands placed on students' brains as they proceed throughout their day. Because nearly every move students make is monitored in school, they cannot take their behavioral choices lightly. (As one sophomore told me, "Between our discussion group time and the time we arrive at our next class, our words can become schoolwide gossip. It's scary sometimes!")

The process of putting ideas together, drawing conclusions, making decisions, and taking action becomes easier for students as their brains grow and create new connections. They become increasingly able to make culturally and socially responsible choices. And since decision-making approaches and criteria can vary among cultures, SEL is necessary for students to be able to handle relationships and work together in diverse environments.

Executive Function Skills

This book focuses on the following executive function skills:

- Impulse inhibition: the process of restraining one's immediate impulses or behavior
- Working memory: the ability to hold and work with information for a short period of time
- Attention and focus: the ability to direct the mind to specific information and stay on task
- Cognitive flexibility: the ability to adapt to changes in plans or to new challenges or to think about multiple concepts simultaneously
- Self-monitoring: the ability to check one's progress toward goals and adjust strategies to meet them; self-awareness and monitoring of thinking processes
- Planning, organization, prioritization, and time management: the ability to design and follow through on a plan in a timely fashion

According to the Center on the Developing Child at Harvard University (2011), "Acquiring the early building blocks of [executive function] skills is one of the most important and challenging tasks of the early childhood years, and the opportunity to build further on these ... is critical to healthy development through middle childhood and adolescence" (p. 1). Remember, these skills are not innate—they must be taught, modeled, and practiced. The Center on the Developing Child (2012) also emphasizes that

- Executive function skills are essential not just in school, but throughout life;
- Relationships are critical to learning and practicing EFS;
- Adults in a student's life can be trained to teach EFS; and
- Teachers need professional development in this area to better understand and provide for student needs.

Students who have difficulty with executive functioning may exhibit any or all of the following characteristics:

- Inability to pay attention
- Impulsive behavior
- Consistent tardiness
- Losing and forgetting things
- Trouble finishing assignments

- Interrupting others
- Getting frustrated easily
- Difficulty switching between tasks
- Having a cluttered workspace
- Responding inappropriately to stress
- Trouble managing emotions
- Difficulty asking for help

Executive function and SEL skills must be developed in tandem since students whose SEL needs are met can't actually learn until they've also honed their EFS. As cognitive neuroscientist Mary Helen Immordino-Yang says, "A lot of teachers . . . have really strong abilities to engage socially with the students, but then it's not enough. You have to go much deeper than that and actually start to engage with students around their curiosity, their interests, their habits of mind through understanding and approaching material to really be an effective teacher" (quoted in Sparks, 2019). Underscoring the point, a study from the University of Virginia (Vitiello et al., 2022) found that "a decrease in the quality of teacher-child interactions and a decrease in teacher-child closeness between preK and kindergarten [is] associated with lower social-emotional and self-regulation skills."

The opposite of executive function is executive dysfunction—"a behavioral symptom that disrupts a person's ability to manage their own thoughts, emotions and actions . . . most common with certain mental health conditions, especially addictions, behavioral disorders, brain development disorders, and mood disorders" (Cleveland Clinic, n.d.). Anyone can suffer from executive dysfunction, and most people do at one time or another. Think of a time when you could barely control your emotions. We've all been there, and sometimes we have students who are often there due to neurodevelopment disorders or adverse childhood experiences. For example, students with ADHD tend to miss assignments, forget to bring materials to class, interrupt others, and fail to complete assignments. Students who have experienced trauma may also have difficulty executing tasks and may be a few years behind their peers neurologically, as trauma can interrupt their brain development (Perry & Winfrey, 2021). According to Nadine Burke Harris, former surgeon general of California, MRIs of students who have had adverse childhood experiences show "a shrinking of the hippocampus [a brain area important for memory and emotional regulation] and increased size of the amygdala, which is the brain's fear center. This can make you hypervigilant—overly sensitive to threats or challenges" (quoted in Bornstein, 2018).

The Neurological Basis of Executive Functions

The frontal lobe of the brain and many of its substructures, like the prefrontal cortex, drive many of our executive functions in the following ways:

- **By appropriately directing our attention and our behaviors.** *Example*: Marnie realizes she is taking too much time in the morning to put on her makeup. She is certain to miss the bus and Mom will be angry. She grabs her makeup bag and puts it in her backpack as she scurries to the bus stop.
- **By linking past experiences to present situations, which is vital for making sound decisions.** *Example*: Kylie wants to use her English period to work with her group on their project, but she knows Mr. Sterling does not like to send students to the library; last class, he wouldn't let another group go, saying they would just goof around. Before she asks Mr. Sterling if they can work in the library, she creates a quick outline with references from the library that they will need. If she can provide all this information, her teacher is more likely to let her group work outside the classroom.
- **By helping us control our emotions.** *Example*: Joaquin does not get asked to work on the 5th grade student council campaign. He is near tears and wants to run out of the room, but instead, he takes several deep breaths and asks Mrs. Hill if there is some other job he can do.
- **By helping us assess our behavior based on feedback and redirect it or try a new strategy that might fill our needs.** *Example*: Chaille didn't have many friends. She tried to strike up conversations with other girls by asking questions like "Where are you going after school?" "What sport are you going to try out for?" and "What did you get on the science quiz?" She soon noticed that her classmates were avoiding her. At first, she wondered why,

but then she overheard Maria and Amber talking in the restroom. Maria said, "Chaille is always asking me questions; I hate being grilled all the time!" Amber replied, "I know, it's so annoying. Why can't she just *talk,* like we all do?" Chaille didn't understand what they meant, so she started listening more closely to her peers' casual conversations. She heard them say things like "I thought the test was hard." "I'm going to get ice cream after school." "Let's go to the library to see if we can find info on our history topic." It clicked with her that their chat was more informal and initiated by observations rather than questions. So Chaille began talking to the girls instead of questioning them and soon made some social inroads.

It is important to remember that since executive function skills rely on the prefrontal cortex, which doesn't fully develop until the ages of 25 to 30, it can take up to that age range for our executive functions to fully develop (Sinclair, 2023). One of our jobs as teachers is to ensure that this development occurs—and the next few chapters of this book provide strategies for doing just that.

Conclusion

Social-emotional learning encompasses five important competencies that schools are weaving into the curriculum. Although SEL encourages academic learning in addition to the social-emotional piece, there are still learners who are struggling, and many educators are concerned about the academic aspect getting short shrift. Research suggests that students' struggles stem from failing to master the executive function skills—including planning, organization, cognitive flexibility, working memory, and impulse inhibition—they need for success. Explicitly teaching EF skills *with* the SEL competencies has the potential to change these students' academic prospects.

2

Impulse Inhibition

Trent was a 7th grader with ADHD. Anytime anyone in the classroom spoke, he just had to respond. Whenever the class was asked to sit down, he just had to stand. Don't get me wrong—I liked Trent. *Everyone* liked Trent, yet we spent a lot of time in the teachers' lounge discussing what to do with him. We knew he was on medication, and it helped with some of his issues, but he still had trouble controlling his impulses.

Eventually I decided to give him a pad of small sticky notes each day. I told him that if, instead of blurting out what was on his mind all the time, he could write it down on a note and stick it to his desk, I would stop by at the end of class and discuss each one with him. At first, he would write 10 notes for every topic and miss most of the class, so we worked on creating abbreviations and concentrating on broad topics rather than every small detail. When I'd stop by his desk at the end of class, he often forgot what he was going to say, but just getting the pad of stickies made him happy for a while. So delayed gratification for Trent was only partially successful. I decided to try a timer with him, using that feature on his smartwatch. We set a guideline that he had to wait 10 minutes between making comments. After 10 days, we increased that wait time to 15 minutes. Since I try to teach lessons in 10-minute chunks, by the time Trent was ready to move and talk, we would be having a brain break, so this worked well, with little disruption.

Take a moment to think about the Trents you have in your classroom. Who are they, and how do you help them?

* * *

Are any of these situations familiar to you?

- You're on a diet, yet you can't stop yourself from having that slice of cake in the teachers' lounge.
- There's background music playing, and you feel an uncontrollable urge to get up and dance.
- As you listen to colleagues discuss how to implement cooperative learning, you find yourself interrupting to add your two cents.
- You promised your child you wouldn't snoop around in her room, but when you pick up her laundry and a note falls out of a pocket, you can't resist reading it.
- You honk your horn when the driver in front of you is moving slower than you'd like.

Each of these scenarios is an example of being unable to inhibit impulsive behaviors. Impulse inhibition goes by many names: response inhibition, delayed gratification, impulse control, self-regulation. When I ask teachers which of the SEL competencies they feel is most important, impulse control is the most common response, and it is probably the most critical executive function skill as well.

What the Research Says

Here are some key findings from the research on impulse inhibition:

- The ventrolateral and dorsolateral regions of the prefrontal context play a crucial role in controlling impulsive behaviors (Mitchell & Potenza, 2014).
- Impulse inhibition develops from childhood through adolescence (Guare et al., 2013).
- Deficits are often associated with attention-deficit/hyperactivity disorder (ADHD) (Barkley, 2020).

- Deficits also contribute to emotional dysregulation (Tull, 2023) as well as to social difficulties (Liu & Li, 2020).
- Cognitive training programs have been shown to help strengthen impulse inhibition (Scionti et al., 2020).
- Inadequate sleep has been shown to compromise executive functions, including impulse inhibition (McCarver-Reyes, 2019).
- Factors related to personality, genetics, and the environment have all been shown to affect impulse inhibition (Bezdjian et al., 2011), as have different cultural contexts (Schmitt et al., 2019).

Ongoing research continues to deepen our understanding of neural mechanisms, developmental trajectories, and practical interventions related to impulse inhibition. The general timeline of development for impulse inhibition is as follows:

- **Early childhood (3–5 years).** Children begin to develop impulse control.
- **Middle childhood (6–12 years).** Children experience significant growth in impulse inhibition, especially around 10 years old. This growth coincides with further development of the prefrontal cortex.
- **Adolescence (13–18 years).** Impulse inhibition continues to develop during this period. Although adolescents are often seen as entirely lacking in impulse inhibition, a more measured view is that teens are suddenly thrown into adult situations that they aren't equipped to handle owing to lack of experience. They may appear to be taking risks when they are actually searching for ways to deal with new situations and simply choosing the wrong approach.
- **Early adulthood (18–25 years).** Young adults continue to hone their ability to control impulses until the full development of the prefrontal cortex around age 25. Adults generally realize that to get and maintain employment, it is necessary to get along with others, which often includes inhibiting impulses.

The Stanford Marshmallow Test

In the famous Stanford marshmallow test of 1970, psychologist Walter Mischel and colleagues offered young children a choice between one marshmallow now or two marshmallows later. The subjects each received a marshmallow and were told that the experimenter was no longer monitoring them. If they waited to eat the marshmallow until the experimenter returned, they would receive two marshmallows. What's most amazing about this simple test is that it seems to have predicted the children's future trajectories. When they were tracked down 14 years after the experiment, those who had resisted impulse and delayed gratification were shown to have handled life more easily. They appeared to be less stressed, dealt with pressure better, and had higher scores on their SATs than their peers who couldn't wait for that second marshmallow (Goleman, 1994).

However, a more recent study calls these conclusions into question. Researchers Tyler Watts, Greg Duncan, and Haonan Quan restaged the marshmallow test with a larger group of subjects more representative of the U.S. population in terms of race, ethnicity, and parents' education and income (Calarco, 2018). The results of this study suggest that a child's ability to delay gratification is correlated to their socioeconomic background. It makes sense that a student who has inadequate food resources would have difficulty waiting for more when something is offered immediately. Physician and author Pamela Cantor, an expert on the science of learning and development and the founder of Turnaround for Children at Arizona State University—an organization that helps train teachers and others on the impact of trauma, neuroplasticity, and the building blocks of learning—explains that children's ability to have self-control is directly related to the context in which they are asked to have that control: If they are in a context with an adult they trust, they are more likely to control their impulses (Sprenger, 2020).

The SEL Connection

Figure 2.1 shows the connections between SEL skills and impulse inhibition.

Consider self-awareness, for example. Maeven is preparing for school one hectic morning. As she fills her backpack with textbooks and last night's homework, she becomes more and more agitated. When her mother approaches her, saying, "Let's get in the car—you've already missed the bus and I don't want you to be late," Maeven retorts, "Get off my back! Can't you see that I'm working on it?!" Her mother replies softly, "What's going on, honey? This is not how you want to start your

Figure 2.1. The SEL Connection to Impulse Inhibition

SEL Skill	Connection to Impulse Inhibition
Self-Awareness	By being aware of their emotions and triggers, students can better recognize situations where they are likely to act impulsively. This awareness is the first step in pausing and thinking before reacting.
Self-Management	Self-management includes skills like impulse control, stress management, and goal setting, which are essential for maintaining attention and focus. Students who can manage their emotions are better able to inhibit their impulses and to stay on task and complete assignments.
Social Awareness	In collaborative settings, social awareness helps students to recognize when they or their peers are losing focus as well as to consider the feelings and perspectives of others before responding impulsively. This understanding fosters a supportive environment where students help one another to stay engaged and attentive.
Relationship Skills	Effective communication and cooperation in group activities require students to inhibit impulsive responses, instead staying focused and attentive to their peers and honing collaboration and conflict resolution skills. These skills ensure that students remain engaged in discussions and activities, enhancing overall group performance.
Responsible Decision Making	Responsible decision making is integral to making thoughtful choices rather than succumbing to immediate, impulsive reactions. Making responsible decisions about how to allocate time and attention is crucial for academic success. Students who practice responsible decision making are better at prioritizing tasks and maintaining focus on important activities.

day." Maeven opens her mouth to spit out another angry remark when she stops and wonders, "Why am I being so mean to Mom? What's wrong with me?" She slumps down as tears stream down her face. She finished her homework and she has all her materials, so why is she so upset? Maeven's mom sits with her for a moment and waits for her daughter to get through this. Maeven realizes that her feelings have gone from anxious to angry to sad. She says, "Mom, I think I started feeling anxious about the essay I wrote last night. I finished it and everything, but I'm not sure I did well enough to get the grade I need to finish with an *A* in Language Arts. I didn't realize it was upsetting me so much. I'm sorry for yelling at you."

We must be able to name our emotions before we can tame them, which requires us to maintain a robust vocabulary of emotion words. According to Mark Brackett, author of *Permission to Feel* (2019), the more nuanced students can be when naming their feelings, the easier it is for them to control them. Consider posting the Emotion Word List in Figure 2.2 as a word wall in your classroom to support students (and in the teachers' lounge to support teachers, too!). Discuss the words with your students and explain the subtle differences among the words in each category. Perhaps students can provide examples from their own experiences.

Mindfulness, breathing, and movement are also helpful: All target the amygdala, allowing it to relax and prepare the brain to be open to handle stress and changes (Taren et al., 2015). Meditation, breathing, and movement strategies abound for students at all age levels (see pp. 101–102 in Appendix A for mindfulness strategies).

Figure 2.2. Emotion Word List

Happy	Sad	Hurt	Confident	Energized
great	depressed	jealous	strong	strong
amused	crushed	betrayed	brave	motivated
delighted	disgusted	wounded	successful	focused
glad	dejected	abused	secure	determined
pleased	desperate	dejected	relaxed	inspired
enthusiastic	upset	let down	comforted	renewed
thankful	frustrated	discouraged	peaceful	vibrant
content	heavy	disappointed	optimistic	vital
gleeful	discouraged	miserable	satisfied	bubbly
lucky	ashamed	lousy	pleased	vivacious
Afraid	**Confused**	**Depressed**	**Helpless**	**Angry**
fearful	upset	unhappy	alone	irritated
terrified	doubtful	miserable	powerless	enraged
suspicious	uncertain	despondent	empty	annoyed
anxious	indecisive	sad	abandoned	upset
nervous	perplexed	down	deserted	hostile
shaky	embarrassed	glum	vulnerable	mad
scared	hesitant	powerless	incapable	livid
worried	shy	guilty	discarded	irate
horrified	muddled	disappointed	forsaken	furious
petrified	puzzled	lousy	weak	hateful

Because this work begins with educators, we need to look at our own behaviors, which have a direct influence on our students. The Southwest Institute for Emotional Intelligence (2018) suggests the following strategies for preventing impulsive behaviors:

- Stop and take a deep breath before reacting to a situation.
- Remember that instant gratification is short-lived and is sometimes about taking the low road. It is better to take the high road and maintain calm and a healthy sense of humor. For example, when it comes to challenging student behavior, a teacher taking the low road might react by trying to control the student ("Sit down and don't say another word!" or "Get out of my classroom right now and go to the office!"), which could hurt their relationship as well as lead to more behavior problems later. In contrast, a teacher taking the high road might say, "You may have a point, and I'd like to talk to you about it after I finish with this."
- Take the time to evaluate your options; sometimes no response is the most powerful response of all.
- Listen to *hear* instead of listening to *respond*. Don't act until you can remove any distractions or remove yourself from them. Your brain needs time to move from automatic reactions to thoughtful ones.
- Leave 10 minutes early to appointments so you have time to practice mindfulness on the way.

Characteristics of Underdeveloped Impulse Inhibition in Students

Some common signs of impulse inhibition difficulties in students include the following:

- **Impatience.** Students may exhibit impatience, struggling to wait their turn during class activities, discussions, or group work.
- **Interruptions.** Students may frequently interrupt the teacher, classmates, or guest speakers during lessons.
- **Lack of understanding.** Students may respond to questions without fully considering or understanding them, so their answers lack depth or coherence.
- **Trouble following instructions.** Students may have problems following directions, misinterpreting or overlooking details.

- **Fidgety behaviors.** Students may frequently get up from their seats, wander around the classroom, or engage in other restless movements.
- **Broken relationships.** Impulsive behaviors can damage relationships with peers, with broader social and academic implications for students.
- **Difficulty planning ahead.** Students may make last-minute decisions without considering the consequences.
- **Inappropriate talk.** Students may make inappropriate or off-topic comments that disrupt the classroom atmosphere.
- **Risky behaviors.** Students may engage in unsafe behaviors without considering the potential consequences.
- **Inconsistent academic performance.** Students may start assignments enthusiastically but struggle to sustain their focus over time.
- **Lack of empathy.** Students may struggle to consider the feelings and perspectives of their peers.
- **Pushback against authority.** Students may impulsively challenge authority figures without considering the potential consequences.

It's important to note that these behaviors can vary in intensity and frequency among students. Additionally, impulse inhibition difficulties may co-occur with other conditions such as ADHD or other executive function challenges.

Recognizing the signs and providing targeted support and interventions can contribute to the social and academic success of your students with impulse inhibition difficulties. In addition, you may wish to administer the Impulse Inhibition Self-Assessment in Figure 2.3. You can initially use this assessment as a class activity, explaining each statement (all are examples of weak impulse inhibition; the self-assessments in subsequent chapters follow the same pattern) or asking for commentary from students and then asking them to fill out the assessment on their own. If you have time to meet with students individually, you could conduct the assessment one-on-one. However you do it, the main goal is to give students time to think about their actions or inactions. Note that if you collect the assessments, you may not get accurate responses, as many students will want to look good in your eyes and give the "right" answer. There's no value in that. Letting students keep them in their folders where they can refer to them may be more helpful.

Figure 2.3. Impulse Inhibition Self-Assessment

Put a check mark in the column that best describes you in these learning situations.	Always	Often	Sometimes	Rarely	Never
I speak out without waiting to be called on.					
If someone is in my way, I push them out of the way.					
I find it hard to wait for things I want.					
I interrupt others when they are speaking.					
I have trouble making choices.					
I do whatever the other kids are doing, even if I don't want to.					
I choose fun things to do instead of homework.					
I take risks.					
I do things without thinking about the outcomes or consequences.					
I have trouble managing my emotions when I am angry or frustrated.					
I do things without planning first.					

Strategies for Younger Students

Following are some strategies for improving impulse inhibition in younger students:

- Provide sticky notes to students who have trouble controlling what they say and when they say it and ask them to write down what they want to share on the notes rather than out loud. If they feel what they have to say is important, they can share it with the teacher at the end of class. (Note that although this strategy was only partially successful for Trent, it works very well for some students!)
- Be sure to post class rules or norms where your students can clearly see them. Feel free to use visuals as well as text and be sure to include rules for controlling impulsive actions (e.g., "Always

raise your hand to ask for help"). Lead your students in compiling the rules before you post them, and go over them often to make sure everyone understands them. Be sure to define each rule (e.g., explain what it means to "use materials appropriately").
- Write the agenda for the day on the board. As items are completed, place a check mark next to them so students can see clearly what is next and what they've accomplished.
- Provide students with time warnings as often as possible (e.g., "You have five minutes to finish your drawing and place it in the art box on my desk").
- Match deadlines to student needs. Some students with impulse inhibition issues will benefit from having additional time to complete a task, while others work better under pressure and are more motivated by a shorter deadline.
- Create a designated area in the classroom where students can take a break to calm down and regain control when they are feeling impulsive. It's important for students to know it's OK to need to calm down and to take the time necessary to do so.
- Develop "social stories" that illustrate appropriate social behaviors in different situations. Social stories usually depict how someone the students' own age experienced and responded to situations. These help students make connections to their own lives and understand the expected responses to and consequences for impulsive behaviors. You can use the story of Trent from the start of this chapter for one of your stories. The Watson Institute offers examples of social stories to use specifically to teach impulse inhibition skills (go to https://www.thewatsoninstitute.org/resource/self-control).
- Offer students choices within reasonable limits. Allowing them to make decisions within a structured framework fosters a sense of autonomy and reduces the chances of impulsive behavior. Limited choices will help some students be more decisive.
- Create a supportive environment for students to express their emotions. Teach them ways to communicate feelings that are appropriate to the classroom environment instead of reacting impulsively.
- Establish consistent daily routines. By helping students feel secure, routines can reduce impulsive behavior.

- Implement a buddy system for students to support one another in making good choices and model positive behavior.
- Offer immediate feedback on impulsive behaviors, emphasizing positive actions and discussing alternative choices. Consistent feedback helps students understand the consequences of their actions.
- Celebrate and acknowledge small victories in impulse control. This can be as simple as saying, "I noticed how you didn't interrupt the conversation. Great work!" or putting a sticky note on a student's desk that says, "I appreciate how you let others speak without interruption!" Positive reinforcement encourages students to continue practicing self-control.
- Maintain open communication with parents. Share strategies you're implementing in the classroom and collaborate on consistent approaches to reinforcing impulse inhibition. Students may behave very differently at home than at school, and you can learn a lot about them from their parents.
- Share stories or examples of positive role models who demonstrate good impulse control. Discuss how these individuals make thoughtful decisions. This can fit right into your curriculum: Literary characters, historical figures, and people from the news are all good places to start.
- Integrate games and activities that require turn taking and patience. Board games, cooperative play, and structured group activities can all promote impulse inhibition.
- Have students engage in group storytelling. This activity helps develop several executive function skills and is particularly good for strengthening impulse control. Either you or a student starts a story, and the group takes turns telling it.
- Have students perform stories. This activity requires students to follow the plot of a story without any deviations. The structure acts as a guide, reducing students' likelihood of acting impulsively.
- Use yoga in the classroom. This is a quiet way to reduce stimulation that requires focused attention. Yoga can also help students to regulate their breathing, which has a calming effect.
- Put on some music and have students move to the rhythm and tempo. This allows them to control their bodies while paying attention to the pace of the music or following others as they speed up or slow down.

- Play music for several seconds while students move around, then stop it at random; whenever the music stops, everyone must freeze. This activity achieves two things: (1) Students watch their peers model the appropriate behavior and follow suit, and (2) students who need it get practice inhibiting their tendency to keep moving.

Consistency, positive reinforcement, and a supportive classroom environment are all key elements in helping younger students develop their impulse inhibition skills. It's important to tailor strategies to student needs and developmental levels.

Strategies for Older Students

Here are some strategies for improving impulse inhibition in older students:

- Encourage students to keep a reflection journal where they write about situations in which they faced challenges related to impulse control, analyze their reactions, and explore alternative responses. If time is an issue, talk to colleagues about sharing a schedule (e.g., students journal in English class on Mondays, in math class on Tuesdays, etc.).
- Explain the idiom "to roll with the punches" and how much less stressful things are when you can control your impulses. Then, make a list of situations that can lead to impulsive behaviors, write them on slips of paper, and put them in a container (e.g., "You studied all night for your test and you only got 10 percent of the answers correct"). Call on a student (or take a volunteer) and ask them to draw a slip of paper out and hand it to you. Read the situation aloud and have the student say how they would respond. If their response demonstrates impulse inhibition (e.g., "Take a deep breath, count to 10, and ask to meet with my teacher to discuss the grade and a retake"), everyone applauds. If it does not (e.g., "Rip up the test and say, 'Forget this stupid class!' and run out"), ask them to try again or ask for a volunteer response. When the game is over, applaud everyone for participating.
- Provide students with social skills training. Programs that teach students about active listening, empathy, and conflict resolution can contribute to impulse control.

- Work with students to develop a classroom contract that outlines expected behaviors and consequences for impulsive actions. Having students participate in the creation of the contract fosters a sense of ownership.
- Analyze examples from news stories, movies, or TV shows in which impulsive decisions lead to significant consequences. Facilitate discussions about the impact of impulsivity on individuals and society.
- Engage students in debates or discussions on topics that require them to consider multiple perspectives before expressing their opinions. This promotes critical thinking while supporting impulse inhibition.
- Institute peer-mentorship programs. It's well known that one of the most powerful ways to learn something is to teach it. Mentoring younger students encourages older students to model positive behaviors, including impulse inhibition.
- Have students engage in community service projects that require planning, organization, and cooperation, all of which support the development of impulse control.
- Have students hold mock job interviews. Mock job interviews help students practice impulse inhibition in communication and decision making, which is crucial for future career success. Students can play the roles of employers and job candidates, both of whom will need to show they can control their impulses.
- Invite guest speakers who can share personal experiences related to impulse control. Hearing from individuals who have faced challenges and learned from them can be impactful. And if the guest speaker's topic relates to the content you're teaching, so much the better.

Consistent implementation and reinforcement of these strategies—and tailoring them to address the specific challenges faced by older students—will help develop and strengthen students' impulse inhibition in various contexts.

Conclusion

Teachers find impulse inhibition one of the most important executive function skills because it's one that strongly affects classroom management and their ability to teach. Simply knowing that it *is* an EFS is helpful, and that the more you model impulse inhibition, the more likely your students are to understand it. Many students have been labeled ADHD because of this executive dysfunction. Explain to your students that every time they manage their emotions, keep themselves from interrupting, or resist any temptation, they are gaining control over their brains. That control will allow them to think clearly, learn more, and have better relationships with others.

3

Working Memory

Jahsolyn needs constant reminders about things. She forgets to turn in her homework and to bring her supplies to class. She also has difficulty following instructions. Her teacher patiently repeats them once, but she's not as patient the second, third, or fourth time. Zion is in the same class and, like Jahsolyn, he has trouble both recalling instructions and copying sentences off the board. He cannot hold on to more than one or two words or numbers at a time, and he is always the last one finished.

We've all had students like Jahsolyn and Zion. We may think of these students as slow, unmotivated, or even lazy, and we may wonder what is going on inside their heads. The truth is, any of us can have similar memory issues. Do any of the following situations sound familiar?

- You walk into the kitchen and don't remember why.
- You've looked all over the house and still can't find your car keys.
- You walk out of the mall and you can't find your car.
- You have to repeat phone numbers to yourself over and over to make sure you have them right.

- You're cooking a recipe you found online and keep having to go back to your laptop or phone because you can't remember the next ingredient.
- You meet someone at a party and can't remember their name 5 minutes later. You meet them again and 10 minutes later you've forgotten their name again.

And how about these examples from the classroom?

- A student reads a chapter in a text but can't remember enough about it to answer questions.
- A student's essay rambles on and misses the point of the topic.
- Students complain about a classmate who doesn't follow the rules of a game.
- A student regularly fails to complete or to bring in their homework.
- A student can't solve math problems without using fingers for counting.
- A student can't recall which steps in a task they've completed and which remain to be finished.

I have been teaching memory courses to people young and old for many years. The fact of the matter is, we *all* need to work on our working memories. There are some things we need to know without looking them up. To work well with others, we must remember things about them. Our students also need to remember the things that will help them get along with their teachers and their classmates, successfully complete their work, and generally navigate their day in school.

What Is Working Memory?

Working memory is a cognitive function that allows us to temporarily hold and manipulate information in our minds. It has been described as a "mental scratchpad" (Jacobson, 2023)—it's where we make a note of ideas, review them, connect them, and correct them. Located in the prefrontal cortex, it is a spot where synthesis can thrive. Working memory is also critical for reasoning, which necessitates holding information and ideas in mind to see how they relate to one another; for creativity, which requires us to see connections between outwardly unconnected ideas; and for analysis, whereby we break things down, examine their components, and recombine them in new and unexpected ways.

What the Research Says

Working memory is limited in time and space. Neurotypical individuals can typically only hold three to five bits of information at a time, and neurodiverse people may hold even fewer (Busch, n.d.). The overall memory process involves a series of steps: encoding, or intake of information; storage, when the information is consolidated into a long-term memory; and, finally, retrieval of that information. Working memory helps us process new information; in addition, when stored information is retrieved, it's placed into working memory.

Encoding involves receiving new information, connecting it to existing information, and then forming a *memory trace*—an initially weak connection in short-term memory that has the potential of being consolidated into long-term memory (Brown et al., 2014). If a learner has difficulty focusing on or attending to new information, or if they can't relate the new information to existing knowledge, encoding will be difficult. When we try to relate information to the lives of our students, we aren't only emphasizing its relevance; we are also helping students make the necessary connections to keep that information in their memory. Once a learner receives new information, the prefrontal cortex holds on to it while they draw from long-term memory to make sense of it. It is important for the learner to keep in mind the purpose of the mental task for which the information is to be used; otherwise, the information may not stick.

Just as important as storing our memories is retrieving them. How many times has a student said to you, "I know it—don't tell me. It's on the tip of my tongue—nope, I can't get it"? Then, the moment they hear the answer, they exclaim, "I knew it!" When retrieval does not come easily, we can become stressed, which can overpower working memory and leave no space for the actual work it was meant to do (Lukasik et al., 2019). This is way too much for working memory—that "scratchpad" is filled with negative thoughts and stress chemicals instead of helpful information. This type of failure leads to frustration and can kill self-confidence.

Working memory has been shown to predict both reading and math competence in students (Diamond, 2014). When students are learning to read, working memory can be particularly taxed: Decoding words slows the brain down and uses up precious memory space. Once a student becomes a fluent reader, no longer having to stop to decode each word, memory frees up substantially. Similarly, to solve math problems, students must be able to hold on to the components of the problem, use previous knowledge, and manipulate those numbers to ascertain the answer. In short, complex thinking requires access to previously stored information, and working memory is the place in the brain where this meeting of old and new information occurs.

Working memory is only one of several memory systems in the brain. These memory systems are complex and can be broadly categorized into several types, each responsible for different aspects of memory storage and retrieval. Following is an overview of the main memory systems and their functions.

1. **Sensory memory.** Sensory memory is the brief storage of sensory information (sight, sound, touch, and so on), lasting between a few milliseconds and a couple of seconds. *Function:* It allows the brain to retain impressions of sensory information after the original stimulus has ceased. Sensory memory acts as a buffer for stimuli received through the senses.

2. **Short-term memory (STM).** Short-term memory holds a small amount of information (about seven items) for a brief period (around 20–30 seconds). *Function:* It is responsible for the temporary storage and manipulation of information necessary for cognitive tasks such as learning, reasoning, and comprehension. STM is crucial for following conversations, solving problems, and making decisions in the moment.

3. **Working memory.** Working memory is a subset of short-term memory that involves the manipulation and processing of information. *Function:* It is used for tasks that require cognitive effort and manipulation of information, such as mental arithmetic, language comprehension, and complex problem solving. It is often divided into components like the *phonological loop* (verbal information), the *visuospatial sketchpad* (visual and spatial information), and the *central executive* (control and coordination).

4. **Long-term memory (LTM).** Long-term memory is the system responsible for storing information for extended periods, ranging

from hours to a lifetime. It is divided into explicit (declarative) memory and implicit (nondeclarative) memory.
- **Explicit (declarative) memory** includes *episodic memory*—the memory of personal experiences and specific events, including the context in which they occurred (e.g., recalling your last birthday)—and *semantic memory,* or the memory of facts, concepts, and general knowledge about the world (e.g., knowing the capital of France).
- **Implicit (nondeclarative) memory** includes *procedural memory* (memory for motor skills and actions, such as riding a bike or typing on a keyboard); *priming* (enhanced ability to identify or process a stimulus due to a previous encounter with it, such as hearing a song and later recognizing it more quickly); and *classical conditioning* (learning through association, such as salivating when you see food).
5. **Emotional memory.** Emotional memory involves the storage and recall of experiences that are associated with strong emotions. *Function:* It is closely linked with the amygdala and helps prioritize and strengthen the memories of emotionally significant events.

Several important brain structures involved in memory include the following:

- **Amygdala:** A structure found in each hemisphere of the brain involved in emotional memory and the emotional enhancement of other types of memory
- **Basal ganglia and cerebellum:** Important for procedural memory (motor learning)
- **Hippocampus:** A structure next to the amygdala essential for the formation and retrieval of explicit memories, especially episodic and spatial memory
- **Prefrontal cortex:** Part of the frontal lobe; crucial for working memory, decision making, and the organization and retrieval of memories

Understanding the various memory systems and their associated brain structures provides insight into how we process, store, and retrieve information, influencing everything from everyday tasks to complex learning and problem solving.

Research shows that exposure to highly stressful early environments is associated with underdeveloped working memory (Vogel & Schwabe, 2016). According to Harvard Health Publishing, "animals that experience prolonged stress have less activity in the parts of their brain that handle higher-order tasks—for example, the prefrontal cortex—and more activity in the primitive parts of their brain that are focused on survival, such as the amygdala" (2021).

Sleep is necessary for learning and memory—especially REM sleep, which helps our brains establish new connections. This is why young people spend more time in this sleep stage than adults. It is also important for problem solving, creativity, and processing emotional memories. When we are upset about something before bed, we usually feel better about it in the morning thanks to REM! During deep sleep, our brains are emptied of the unimportant memories in the hippocampus and important memories are selected for long-term storage. There is a direct relationship between the amount of deep sleep students get and how well they perform on a memory test the next day (Attia, 2023). Conversely, lack of sleep causes stress hormones to be released, which occludes working memory.

The following is a general timeline of working memory development:

- **Early childhood (3–5 years).** Working memory has been developing since students were six months old, but during early childhood, students are better able to hold things in mind. Some can hold four bits of information simultaneously.
- **Middle childhood (6–12 years).** Students can begin to plan how they will complete a complex sequence of actions. By the end of this stage, working memory capacity is around five pieces of information, which is on par with adult working memory.
- **Adolescence (13–18 years).** This stage sees significant improvement in working memory. Students are able to hold many bits of information, chunk information, and use multiple strategies to retain information.
- **Early adulthood (18–25 years).** During these prime memory years, the prefrontal cortex will be developed and reach full capacity. Decline can begin between ages 25 and 30.

The SEL Connection

Figure 3.1 shows the connections between SEL skills and working memory.

As deWilde and colleagues (2016) note, "Working memory is an important factor in children's social development" because "adequate processing of social information is essential for the development of children's social cognition and behavior." Underdeveloped working memory has been associated with difficulty handling social situations. As students' social worlds widen, they must spend more time in situations that require social skills that depend on working memory. It's also the case that poor social situations can diminish working memory. The central SEL competencies of self-awareness, self-management,

Figure 3.1. The SEL Connection to Working Memory

SEL Skill	Connection to Working Memory
Self-Awareness	Self-awareness helps students understand how their emotional states affect their ability to focus and remember information. Being aware of their strengths and areas for improvement can help them develop strategies to enhance their working memory.
Self-Management	Strong self-management skills enable students to maintain focus and control impulses that might interfere with their ability to hold and manipulate information in working memory. Techniques such as goal setting and self-monitoring are part of self-management and support utilization of working memory.
Social Awareness	Classwide social awareness can indirectly bolster working memory by creating a supportive and empathetic classroom environment. When students feel understood and supported, they are more likely to be engaged and focused, which can enhance their working memory.
Relationship Skills	Students with strong relationship skills rely on their working memory to recall important information about others, such as their preferences, experiences, and emotions. Effective communication and collaboration often require holding information in mind, such as remembering instructions or contributions from peers.
Responsible Decision Making	Making responsible decisions often requires considering various pieces of information and potential outcomes. Working memory is crucial for holding this information in mind while evaluating options and making choices.

social awareness, relationship management, and decision making all rely on working memory.

Characteristics of Underdeveloped Working Memory in Students

Some common signs of working memory difficulties in students include the following:

- **Difficulty following instructions.** Students may struggle to remember and follow multistep instructions. Both at school and at home, they might become overwhelmed when presented with several tasks at once, leading to confusion and incomplete assignments.
- **Forgetfulness.** Forgetfulness is a hallmark of working memory challenges. Students may frequently forget details of assignments, upcoming events, or other important information, even if they've just been introduced to it. At home they may forget to have permission slips signed or forget to do chores.
- **Inattentiveness.** Students may appear inattentive or easily distracted during lessons as they grapple with the cognitive load of processing and retaining information.
- **Difficulty organizing thoughts.** Students may struggle to organize their thoughts logically, in both written and verbal communication.
- **Difficulty with reading comprehension.** Reading comprehension relies on the ability to hold and manipulate information in working memory. Students may find it challenging to understand and remember the sequence of events, characters, or key details in a text if their working memories are weak.
- **Difficulty with mathematics.** Working memory is essential for tasks involving mathematical calculations and problem solving. Students may have difficulties remembering and applying mathematical formulas or recalling relevant information when trying to solve math problems.
- **Delayed processing.** Students may experience delays in processing information and need extra time to understand instructions, formulate responses, or complete assignments.
- **Difficulty with transitions.** Switching between tasks or activities can be challenging for students with underdeveloped working

memory, which can lead to disruptions in their workflow and trouble adjusting to changes in classroom routines.
- **Reliance on inefficient learning strategies.** Students may rely on less effective learning strategies due to working memory limitations. For example, they might have difficulties using mnemonic devices or other memory aids that could enhance their learning. Consider the example of the student near the beginning of the chapter who counted on their fingers because they couldn't hold or picture the information in their working memory.
- **Difficulty with long-term memory retention.** Students may face challenges retaining information for future use, affecting their ability to build on previous knowledge and skills.
- **Reduced problem-solving skills.** Students may have difficulty holding and manipulating information while solving problems.
- **Avoidance of complex tasks.** Students may avoid tasks that require significant mental effort or involve complex instructions. This can hinder their academic progress and limit their engagement in challenging activities.

Recognizing the signs and providing targeted support and interventions can contribute to the social and academic success of your students with working memory difficulties. In addition, you may wish to use the Working Memory Self-Assessment in Figure 3.2.

Strategies for Younger Students

Following are some strategies for improving working memory in younger students:
- Minimize the burden on working memory by offloading new learning onto paper, sticky notes, pictures, signs, cues, and other such resources.
- Limit distractions. As much as we love to have bright, colorful rooms filled with posters and pictures, the visual stimulation can be very distracting. Look around your room to see if you can determine what you might modify, change, or remove to limit distractions.
- Engage students in "digital span tasks." Give them three numbers, then ask them to repeat them or write them down several seconds later. If the numbers are correct, give students four numbers.

Figure 3.2. Working Memory Self-Assessment

Put a check mark in the column that best describes you in these learning situations.	Always	Often	Sometimes	Rarely	Never
I constantly misplace my phone and waste time every day looking for it.					
I am accused of not listening when I don't get tasks done.					
When I have something to ask my teacher, I wait for them to finish speaking and then forget what I wanted to ask.					
When speaking with friends, I forget what they were saying before I can comment on it.					
I forget to bring home items I need to get my homework done.					
When I have a task with several steps, I forget many of the final steps.					
I rush around to get ready for school, but I am still late.					
I forget what I have read when I finish reading.					
I have trouble retelling a story right after the teacher has read it to me.					
I enjoy and want to play sports, but I forget the rules of the game.					
Even when something is important, I often forget it.					

Repeat the process until you are using seven numbers. You can also use letters, lists of items, and so on. These tasks exercise students' working memory simply by providing practice time for them. Many of our executive function skills require practice (Mathy et al., 2018).

- Shorten assignments. Consider giving students 5 problems to work at home instead of 10 or more. Spelling tests could also be limited to 5–10 words. Students will feel less overwhelmed and stressed, and

you will still be giving them ample opportunity to build their content knowledge and working memory.
- Provide information in multiple formats. For example, you certainly have students who remember better what they read rather than what they listen to; if feasible, others may like to have a video they can refer back to when needed. Try a variety of modes.
- Don't rely on verbal instructions only—combine them with visual cues whenever possible. The magic of working memory is its ability to hold on to information, manipulate it, and then store it. Disseminating information in a verbal format saves time, but it doesn't always give students time to absorb it. When you combine the verbal with the visual, you are giving students a second chance to catch on.
- When you *do* use verbal instructions, pick a student at random to repeat them, and cue students to write down their own reminders if they think they won't remember.
- Chunk information. Divide your lessons into segments that don't exceed your students' attention spans.
- According to Medina (2018), no matter what ages your students are, you should give them a "brain break" every 10 minutes or so.
- Have students complete KWL charts. Listing what they *know* about a topic, what they *want* to know about it, and what they have *learned* about it can help students reinforce working memory.
- Supply students with visual checklists—for example, the day's agenda, steps to solving a problem, the characters or plot of a story, and so on. These are especially helpful for students who require a visual cue or who may still have struggles with reading fluency.
- Break tasks down into subroutines. This allows students to tackle just one component at a time, lightening the load on their working memory.
- Provide students with regular reminders of what they need to do next.
- Ask students to repeat back new information they have learned and help them connect it with what they already know. This kind of retrieval practice is necessary to cement information in long-term memory.

- Instead of asking students what they did over break or during the weekend, ask them what they *learned*. This activity serves as both relationship building and retrieval practice.
- Encourage students to ask questions if they're feeling lost.
- Teach students how to create and use their own memory aids.
- Have students tell one another stories, as storytelling appears to be more effective than reading a story at developing working memory and attention (Diamond, 2021). Having students take turns telling a story is especially helpful.
- Have students develop and engage in self-talk, which you can model through think-aloud activities. Use think-alouds often, especially when you are problem-solving and trying to draw connections between existing knowledge and new learning. You may ask students to repeat what you say or put it into their own words.
- Have students read books in pairs, alternating reading and listening roles.

Strategies for Older Students

Following are some strategies for improving working memory in older students:

- Use think-pair-share activities, being sure to give students time to retrieve information from long-term memory and hold it in working memory as they share. These also increase social awareness, relationship skills, and decision-making skills.
- As an exit ticket, ask students to write down at least two things they remember from class. Every time they do this, they're ensuring faster retrieval of that information down the line.
- Give students practice tests so they can rehearse retrieving information from their long-term memory.
- Training and practice have been shown to improve working memory in as little as five days (Takeuchi et al., 2011), so consider having students engage in memory-training activities. One well-known memory-training technique is the Dual N-Back game, in which the player looks at a computer screen on which squares randomly appear with a voice saying a specific letter. After several squares and letters

are given, a question pops up and asks which location and letter was last. Then the game becomes more difficult, as the player is asked for the location and letter that was second to last, fourth to last, and so on. An activity like this trains and changes the brain.
- Every day or week, ask students to write about what they learned the previous day or week in their notebooks or in a graphic organizer such as a mind map or concept map. Then follow this up with small-group or whole-class discussion. This is helpful for kids who were absent or simply missed the point of a lesson, and it's a great way for students to practice retrieval. The discussion portion also builds social awareness, relationship skills (especially in the small-group setting), and decision-making skills.
- When giving a unit test, attach a blank sheet on which students can write anything they know about the topic of the exam. Students who may not have known all the answers still have an opportunity to show you what they know. Whether you average this information into the grade is optional, but it provides students with robust memory-retrieval practice.

Conclusion

Take the time to help students develop their working memory through mnemonic devices, digital span tasks, and other strategies mentioned in this chapter. You can also teach students about the different kinds of memory systems. The more kids know about their brains, the better they will use them!

4

Attention and Focus

Kerrin was one of the finest students at Millard Middle School. She always did her homework, answered questions in class, did community service work, and raised money for the Millard Student Council by organizing car washes and donut sales. Kerrin did all those things—until suddenly she didn't. Her teachers started to notice that Kerrin's grades were slipping. She missed several Student Council meetings and seldom raised her hand in class. When asked about missing assignments, she said she had trouble getting to them because she had to take care of her family.

The school counselor, June Hensley, made an appointment to meet with Kerrin and her parents, but they didn't show up. This red flag led to a home visit, where June found that many things had recently changed in Kerrin's life. Her grandmother, who had been helping support the family, had moved into a nursing home, Kerrin's dad had been laid off, and tensions were high at home. How could poor Kerrin be expected to raise money for the school when her family could barely make ends meet? And how could she focus on anything else when she was so worried about her family falling apart? When June found out about the daily trauma Kerrin was facing, she realized the girl needed some coping strategies.

Why do some kids always pay attention while others are bored or overwhelmed and act out? This chapter discusses the root causes of attention and focus difficulties in students and strategies to address them in the classroom.

* * *

There are three broad categories of attention:

- **Sustained attention:** The ability to maintain focus and concentration on a single task over an extended period; what Csikszentmihalyi (2008) refers to as a state of flow
- **Selective attention:** The ability to focus on a specific aspect of the environment while ignoring other stimuli
- **Divided attention:** The ability to shift between tasks and process information from multiple sources

Research by Microsoft (Marks, 2023) further divides attention into the following four quadrants:

- **Focus:** High engagement, high challenge (e.g., an open-ended assignment that provides the opportunity to collaborate with others)
- **Rote:** High engagement, low challenge (e.g., a fun but not especially rigorous or relevant activity)
- **Bored:** Low engagement, low challenge (e.g., a boring, easy review worksheet)
- **Frustrated:** Low engagement, high challenge (e.g., a challenging lab that students are not adequately prepared for)

It is thought that the attention span of children is approximately two to three minutes for each year of age (Ward, 2020) (see Figure 4.1). "To keep students engaged, you must win the battle for their attention every 10 minutes," writes neuroscientist and ASCD author John Medina (2020). "Every 10 minutes I use what I call a 'hook' to refocus my audience on my topic or message. I also organize my material in a hierarchical fashion, because that is how the brain processes information."

Attention and focus play crucial roles in student's learning and contribute to the following aspects of their educational experience:

- Information acquisition
- Class participation

- Task completion
- Memory and retrieval
- Problem solving
- Time management
- Reading comprehension
- Test performance
- Social interactions
- Classroom behavior
- Motivation and persistence
- Self-regulation
- Participation in extracurricular activities
- Critical thinking
- Innovation and creativity

Figure 4.1. Average Attention Span by Age

Age	Average Attention Span
5	10–14 minutes
6	12–18 minutes
7	14–21 minutes
8	16–24 minutes
9	18–27 minutes
10	20–30 minutes
11	22–33 minutes
12	24–36 minutes
13	26–39 minutes
14	28–42 minutes
15	30–45 minutes
16	32–48 minutes
17	34–51 minutes
18	36–54 minutes

Source: From "What are normal attention spans for children?" by C. M. Ward, 2020, *The Kid's Directory Family Resource Guide*, https://www.kids-houston.com/normal-attention-spans-for-kids.

What the Research Says

The brain's attention system develops gradually between the first year of life and young adulthood (Guare et al., 2013; Willis & Willis, 2020). Attention and focus are closely related cognitive processes that play crucial roles in perception, learning, and cognitive performance. Although the terms are often used interchangeably, focus is actually a specific aspect of attention involving sustained and concentrated mental effort. Characteristics of focus include intensity and the total exclusion of anything distracting. Students are more likely to block out irrelevant stimuli if they find the task at hand interesting, they are motivated to perform it, and it is neither too challenging nor too easy to complete.

Research shows that young children with underdeveloped attention systems do not do well in elementary classrooms with a lot of decorations that are extraneous to learning. One study found that children "were more distracted by the visual environment, spent more time off task, and demonstrated smaller learning gains when the walls [of their classroom] were highly decorated than when the decorations were removed" and that "young children have more attentional control if they are in a classroom where the walls are bare" (Fisher et al., 2014).

As teachers, we are competing with video games and social media for our students' attention. However, there is good news in this area: Research suggests that action video games can improve cognitive functions, including attention (Sampalo et al., 2023).

The general timeline of development for attention and focus is as follows:

- **Early childhood (3–5 years).** Sustained attention begins to develop, enabling children to complete a five-minute chore and sit through the reading of one or two picture books.
- **Middle childhood (6–12 years).** Students' attention span and ability to focus continue to grow; they can spend a limited amount of time on homework (20–30 minutes) and sit through a meal.
- **Adolescence (13–18 years).** Adolescents can work on homework for 60–90 minutes with breaks and work on projects for up to two hours with breaks.

- **Early adulthood (18–25 years).** Young adults can pace themselves and self-monitor so they know when they are no longer able to focus or attend and can set realistic goals for attending to something they care about.

Attention and Trauma

Students who have experienced trauma may exhibit heightened states of arousal and hypervigilance, resulting in difficulty maintaining sustained attention (Perry & Szalavitz, 2007). They may also

- Experience intrusive thoughts or memories that interrupt their concentration (van der Kolk, 2015);
- Develop avoidance strategies that interfere with their ability to engage in tasks that require them to focus (Minahan, 2019); and
- Have dissociative episodes during which attention may be compromised (van der Kolk, 2015).

Attention and Poverty

The stressors associated with living in poverty can negatively impact attention and contribute to chronic distractibility in students (Sleek, 2015). Poverty is also linked to a higher risk of nutritional deficiencies, which can have long-lasting effects on attention and concentration. Students in poverty may be exposed to environmental toxins that impact brain development, and disruptions in students' home lives may compromise their ability to focus and engage in learning (Blair & Raver, 2016).

The SEL Connection

Figure 4.2 shows the connection between SEL skills and attention and focus.

Characteristics of Underdeveloped Attention and Focus in Students

Attention and focus problems can affect various aspects of daily life, and the specific challenges may differ from person to person. Some of

Figure 4.2. The SEL Connection to Attention and Focus

SEL Skill	Connection to Attention and Focus
Self-Awareness	Self-awareness helps students to notice when their attention is waning or when they are becoming distracted. By being aware of these moments, students can employ strategies to regain focus and sustain their attention on the task at hand.
Self-Management	Self-management includes skills like impulse control, stress management, and goal setting, which are essential for maintaining attention and focus. Students who can manage their emotions and impulses are better able to stay on task and complete assignments.
Social Awareness	In collaborative settings, social awareness helps students to recognize when they or their peers are losing focus. This understanding can foster a supportive environment where students help one another to stay engaged and attentive.
Relationship Skills	Relationship skills supply the emotional support necessary for maintaining attention and focus. Effective communication and cooperation in group activities require students to stay focused and attentive to their peers. Strong relationship skills ensure that students remain engaged in discussions and activities, enhancing overall group performance.
Responsible Decision Making	Students who practice responsible decision making are better at prioritizing tasks and maintaining focus on important activities. Making responsible decisions about how to allocate time and attention is crucial for academic success.

the more common signs of attention and focus difficulties in students include the following:

- **Daydreaming.** Students may appear to be staring into space or not engaging in class or at home.
- **Distractibility.** Students may have their attention disrupted by external stimuli such as noises, movements, or objects in the classroom.
- **Incomplete or inaccurate assignments.** Students may begin assignments and never finish them (or finish them but not turn them in) and have a tendency to make careless mistakes.
- **Difficulty following instructions.** Students may struggle to follow the steps for completing tasks properly and require frequent repetition.

- **Restlessness.** Students may tend to fidget, tap their fingers, or shift in their seats.
- **Forgetfulness.** Students may have trouble remembering to bring necessary materials to class or be unable to recall important details about a lesson.
- **Inconsistent academic performance.** Students may go through cycles of high achievement followed by low performance.
- **Lack of participation.** Students may avoid taking part in class discussions or activities.
- **Difficulty organizing tasks.** Students may struggle to maintain an effective schedule and keep track of materials.
- **Procrastination.** Students may delay starting assignments or studying until the last minute.
- **Impulsivity.** Students may have difficulty inhibiting inappropriate behaviors such as blurting out answers or acting without thinking.
- **Difficulty sustaining effort.** Students may quickly lose interest in tasks and appear to give up easily.
- **Relationship difficulties.** Students may have trouble maintaining positive relationships with peers, often owing to things like inattentiveness during conversations, forgetting dates or events that are important to their classmates, or failing to do their part for a group project.
- **Goal setting and achievement.** Students may find it overly challenging to set and meet long-term objectives.
- **Sleep disturbances.** Students may have difficulty controlling their thoughts and subsequently winding down at night, which can cause sleep interruptions.

It's important to note that these signs can indicate a variety of factors other than attention and focus dysfunction, including learning disabilities, emotional challenges, and temporary lack of engagement. If these issues significantly interfere with daily functioning, teachers, parents, and, if necessary, healthcare professionals should work together to identify the underlying causes. Recognizing the signs and providing targeted support and interventions can contribute to the social and academic success of your students with attention and focus difficulties. In addition, you may wish to use the Attention and Focus Self-Assessment in Figure 4.3.

Figure 4.3. Attention and Focus Self-Assessment

Put a check mark in the column that best describes you in these learning situations.	Always	Often	Sometimes	Rarely	Never
I get distracted when there are background noises.					
My homework space is cluttered and disorganized.					
I have a hard time completing tasks without getting sidetracked.					
I have a hard time completing boring tasks.					
I have a hard time concentrating when I am talking on the phone, especially if the TV is on.					
When reading a text or story, I lose the thread and need to reread parts.					
I lose track of my work.					
I lose my focus often and don't know how to get back on track.					
I check my phone every few minutes.					
I tend to stop working on something before I finish it.					

Strategies for Younger Students

Improving attention and focus in younger students involves a combination of environmental, instructional, and supportive strategies. Following are some strategies for improving attention and focus in younger students:

- Establish structured daily routines. These provide a sense of predictability for your students, helping to keep their stress levels low and their attention focused on the work at hand.
- Clearly communicate transitions between activities. Sometimes the brain needs concrete information to switch focus appropriately. Get everyone's attention before asking them to transition to a new activity.

- Ensure a distraction-free environment. In addition to ensuring that any wall decorations serve a learning purpose, arrange seating to reduce visual and auditory distractions. If you know certain students cannot help but stare out the window during lessons, seat them away from the window.
- Allow short breaks for physical activity to help release excess energy. This helps students re-focus their attention when they return to the lesson. Consider also integrating movement into lessons as a way to hold students' attention (e.g., if you're teaching students about the different types of angles, pair them up and have them search the room for examples).
- Because novelty invites attention, incorporate a mix of teaching methods, including hands-on activities, discussions, and interactive lessons, and use a variety of materials to keep lessons interesting. Modeling clay is an enduring favorite in many classrooms. (Anything that students create using it should be small enough to fit on a paper plate.) Playing with a material like this is relaxing as well as engaging.
- Foster a participatory classroom environment by alternating among pair, small-group, and whole-class discussions. This provides both novelty and the opportunity to interact with other students.
- Seek input from students' families on successful attention-getting strategies they use at home, and share strategies that work in the classroom with families. For example, when I discovered that using a timer at school helped a 5th grader extend her focus time, I shared the strategy with her parents, who began using the same method at home.
- Use guided imagery. Have students close their eyes as you read a scene to them or play a recording. This will help them focus on what they're hearing to get the "movie" playing in their mind.
- Implement the "four-corner" activity. As you begin a new unit, think of four different ways in which students may demonstrate their knowledge. Hang a sign in each corner of your room with the four options. Explain each option to your class and then give them 10 seconds to go to the corner they're most comfortable with. Each corner group can then discuss how this approach might look.

If a student has a change of heart after this discussion, they may choose a different corner. Activities that offer choices build student engagement, which naturally promotes focus, since students have more buy-in.
- Use attention-grabbing signal phrases like "hocus pocus, everybody focus" and "mac and cheese, everybody freeze," or have the class come up with their own.
- Play Follow the Leader. In this activity, students must watch and listen closely to the leader as they make moves. This activity also provides the movement that many students require to release the dopamine they need to focus. Examples of this activity include well-known games like Red Light, Green Light and Simon Says.

Strategies for Older Students

Here are some effective strategies for older students:
- Allow students to create or seek the learning environment that works best for them. You may ask your students the following questions:
  – Where do you do your best work?
  – What helps keep you on track?
  – What do you find distracting?
  – What pulls you off track?

  Use students' answers to these questions to set up an environment that is conducive to attention and focus for most of your students. Do what you can to ensure they feel like they belong and their success is important to you.
- Be sure to monitor and control access to digital devices during instructional time.
- Chunk your lessons into digestible and meaningful bits of information so students can attend to the material more easily. Ask yourself questions such as these:
  – Is a 10-minute lecture going to be productive for my students?
  – At what point should I be quiet and let students talk to maintain their attention?
  – At what point in a lesson does students' attention typically begin to drift?

- Greet your students at the door to explain what they can expect to learn in class and direct their attention toward the content. Emotions are contagious, so if you appear excited about the class, you may transfer that excitement to students.
- Maintain eye contact with and physical proximity to students to ensure they are on track.
- Consider the time of the day and how it might affect students' attention and focus. Prior to lunch and in the late afternoon, you may have students who are distracted by hunger or whose insulin levels are crashing; providing them with a snack may help them pay attention in class. Similarly, students may be tired at the very end of the day; to get their homeostatic rhythm going, consider having them move around.
- Promote the importance of sleep, as lack of it can seriously affect attention levels.
- As with younger students, capitalizing on the power of novelty can work wonders. For example, change the way you begin a lesson, post an unusual item on your whiteboard or bulletin board, or walk into class wearing a hat or a costume. As a caveat, none of these attention-getters will be meaningful without relevance, so make sure they are not isolated one-offs but grounded in the lesson or related to students' lives in some way. Here's an example from a colleague: "I always switch things up for seventh period. Last week, I turned all their chairs upside down and told them they had to stand and earn their seats. I had simple questions about the content we were covering. I'd ask a question and they could raise their hands and wait to be called on to answer. Plus, I told them I might be repeating questions, so they listened as each question was answered. Every tired kid in that class just wanted to answer and sit down! It was great retrieval practice for them and kept them focused. In fact, it worked so well that I think I will do the same thing before tests in class!"

For both older and younger students, mindfulness can help support attention and focus. Check out Appendix A for some mindfulness strategies (pp. 101–102).

Conclusion

We struggle to get students' attention at times, and students struggle to focus for extended periods. But there are many strategies to try to keep students attending and focusing. Being aware of kids' attention span at different ages is helpful for designing lessons as well as for giving students brain breaks. With the help of social-emotional learning, students are better able to attend and focus as they are more aware of how they are feeling as well as what they need to be focusing on.

5

Cognitive Flexibility

Chad appeared to be an easygoing student. He worked well with other classmates and always finished his homework and turned it in on time. Because he liked to be the first in line for lunch, he always made sure he had his materials put away so he could rush up to the door.

After a few weeks of observing Chad's routine, his classmate Henry figured out how to be first in line. He'd take a pencil up to the sharpener, which happened to be close to the door, and the moment time was called, he'd be right there. This infuriated Chad, who was now second in line. He tried to push Henry out of the way, yelling, "That's my spot! I'm always first!" "Not today," Henry said with a smirk. At that, Chad lashed out, slamming Henry against the door.

Though it may not seem like a big deal to us, Chad viewed no longer being first in line as a big change to his day-to-day routine. Over time, using many of the strategies in this chapter, Chad slowly became less rigid.

What the Research Says

Cognitive flexibility can be defined as the ability to rapidly and efficiently adapt one's thinking and behavior to match the needs of different situations, including new environments, data, and points of view (Moore & Malinowski, 2009). We actually do this more often than you might think: When we say we're doing several things "at the same time," what we really mean is that we're alternating between multiple undertakings in quick succession. According to Judy Willis (2016a), aspects of cognitive flexibility include the following:

- Open-minded evaluation of different opinions, perspectives, and points of view
- Willingness to risk mistakes
- Consideration of multiple ways to solve problems
- Engagement in learning, discovery, and problem solving with innovative creativity (para. 2)

The anterior cingulate gyrus is the brain structure that allows us to focus on one thing and then shift focus to something else (Amen et al., 2019). Just as a gear shifter in a car that gets stuck in reverse makes it difficult to get into drive and go where we want to go, an overactive anterior cingulate gyrus can result in our being stuck and unable to shift to a different focus. As the brain matures, it becomes easier to get unstuck. Being able to notice when we are stuck is key. Cognitive flexibility helps with this ability to shift and develops gradually in the brain throughout childhood, adolescence, and into early adulthood, with different aspects of this function maturing at different rates depending on both genetic and environmental factors. The general timeline of development is as follows:

- **Early childhood (3–5 years).** Basic cognitive flexibility skills evolve, with children beginning to demonstrate the ability to shift between tasks.
- **Middle childhood (6–12 years).** Children learn to adapt to changes in routine and to understand multiple perspectives in social interactions; their problem-solving abilities become more sophisticated, and they are better able to consider alternative solutions.
- **Adolescence (13–18 years).** Significant improvements in abstract thinking, problem solving, and the ability to consider more complex concepts occur. Adolescents experience greater flexibility adapting to new situations and shifting between tasks.

- **Early adulthood (18–25 years).** Young adults typically demonstrate advanced problem-solving skills and adaptability and are able to handle even more complex cognitive tasks. The prefrontal cortex continues to develop until one's mid-20s (National Institute of Mental Health, 2023).

It's important to note that individual differences exist, and not all students follow the same developmental trajectory. Some factors that can influence cognitive flexibility development include the following:

- Genetic predisposition
- Exposure to varied learning experiences, supportive interactions, opportunities for problem solving, and a stimulating environment
- Educational experiences that challenge and engage students in activities promoting critical thinking and problem solving
- Positive social interactions and exposure to diverse perspectives

The SEL Connection

Figure 5.1 shows the connection between SEL skills and cognitive flexibility.

Characteristics of Underdeveloped Cognitive Flexibility in Students

The Stroop test is a common test for cognitive inflexibility. Participants are asked to read a variety of color words that are written in a color different from what the text says (e.g., the word *red* written in green, the word *blue* written in brown). The words are repeated several times, and the colors are random. In the first round, participants are asked to read the words as they are written, then in the second round they are asked to say the color of each word. We are used to reading what a word says, not naming its color, and our brains have to resist the impulse to do otherwise. Individuals with underdeveloped cognitive flexibility tend to have the greatest difficulty with the Stroop test. When I give workshops on executive function skills, I administer the Stroop test as a way for educators to experience cognitive inflexibility, so they can better understand what their students may be experiencing. I have also given the test

Figure 5.1. The SEL Connection to Cognitive Flexibility

SEL Skill	Connection to Cognitive Flexibility
Self-Awareness	Being self-aware helps students recognize when they need to shift their thinking or adapt their strategies. Self-awareness allows for better understanding and regulation of emotions, which can facilitate smoother transitions between different tasks or perspectives.
Self-Management	Good self-management skills help students stay calm and focused when faced with changes or unexpected challenges. This control over one's responses is crucial for adapting to new information and adjusting plans accordingly.
Social Awareness	Social awareness allows students to consider multiple viewpoints and respond appropriately in social contexts. This empathy and understanding can lead to more flexible thinking and better problem solving in group settings.
Relationship Skills	Effective communication and collaboration often require the ability to adjust one's approach and thinking to accommodate others. This adaptability is a key aspect of cognitive flexibility.
Responsible Decision Making	Responsible decision making involves evaluating multiple options and potential outcomes, which requires flexible thinking. Being able to shift perspectives and consider different consequences is essential for making well-informed decisions.

to students to help them understand their brains and the brains of their classmates.

Cognitive inflexibility manifests in students in various ways, affecting their ability to adapt to different cognitive tasks, perspectives, or learning and social situations. Here are some common signs of cognitive inflexibility in students:

- **Difficulty with transitions, changes in routine, and unpredictability.** Students struggle with transitioning between activities and changes in routine. This can be especially true for kids who are living in unpredictable environments where adults don't always follow through on their promises. Students may be thrown off by any change in routine and be reluctant to participate in activities if there is any deviation. Their whole day can be derailed by a fire drill or even by something as small as the teacher not taking the lunch count before having kids turn in their homework.

- **Rigidity in thinking.** Students have a rigid, "my way or the highway" approach to problems, which can lead to difficulty working in pairs or groups. Students who are labeled as "not playing well with others" may be suffering from cognitive inflexibility.
- **Resistance to new information.** Students may resist learning new concepts, instead clinging to old beliefs. They may even go so far as to withdraw or avoid interacting with new information.
- **Difficulty solving problems.** Students may struggle with open-ended tasks or ambiguous answers.
- **Difficulty adapting to different communication styles.** Students may not understand the various ways people can communicate in different social contexts (e.g., taking turns speaking and listening during class discussions versus interrupting during more casual conversations). Students may also have trouble picking up on non-verbal cues or irony. (Note that sarcasm is not appropriate in the classroom.)
- **Resistance to constructive feedback.** Students may respond defensively to feedback that suggests taking an alternative approach to a problem.
- **Difficulty transferring knowledge and skills.** Students may have trouble transferring information from one context to another (e.g., applying math skills in ELA class).

These signs can also indicate factors including neurodevelopmental conditions, learning disabilities, and environmental stressors. Identifying and addressing these challenges early can allow for the implementation of targeted strategies and interventions to support students' cognitive flexibility in the classroom. Collaborating with educators, specialists, and parents can help create individualized plans that meet students' specific needs. In addition, you may wish to use the Cognitive Flexibility Self-Assessment in Figure 5.2.

Strategies for Younger Students

Supporting cognitive flexibility in younger students involves helping them adapt to new situations, shift their thinking, collaborate with others who have different perspectives, and approach problems from

Figure 5.2. Cognitive Flexibility Self-Assessment

Put a check mark in the column that best describes you in these learning situations.	Always	Often	Sometimes	Rarely	Never
I avoid new and unusual situations.					
I am uncomfortable when plans change.					
I hate it when I am interrupted.					
Negative feedback makes me angry.					
I don't like to try new activities.					
I only want to do one thing at a time.					
I don't enjoy hearing opinions that differ from my own.					
I don't do well handling unpredictable situations or changes to my routine.					
When things don't work out, I am lost rather than having a Plan B in place.					

different angles. Following are some strategies for improving cognitive flexibility in younger students:

- Use visual schedules or timers to help students anticipate transitions and changes in activities.
- Warn students of upcoming changes in schedule and give them time to adjust. Provide a visual countdown to signal upcoming changes, reducing anxiety and enhancing preparation.
- Integrate games and activities that involve rule changes or variations, such as card games that require matching by either suit or number, like gin rummy or UNO. Improvisational games that require players to react to audience comments can help develop cognitive flexibility as well.
- To challenge and strengthen cognitive flexibility, implement activities that involve following rhythmic patterns, such as clapping or

drumming. For instance, if you lead students in a pattern of two claps and two stomps three times in a row and then change the pattern to three claps and one stomp, students' brains must be flexible enough to pivot quickly and make the change.

- Share stories or create scenarios that involve characters adapting to unexpected changes. For example, students love to hear how inventors had to continually change their strategies to design the perfect product. Discuss alternative solutions to problems and encourage children to generate creative ideas.
- Experiment with flexible seating options in the classroom to allow for movement and changes in perspective. This allows students to practice adjusting to new situations.
- Have students create and present social stories that encourage cognitive flexibility by modeling how to adapt to new experiences or navigate social interactions. Here's an example:

> I can be flexible. Sometimes I don't want to be flexible, but I know I can. To be flexible, I will need to know ahead of time what is going to happen. If you post a schedule, that will help me see how flexible I need to be. If I have trouble being flexible, I can take a deep breath, count to 10, ask for help, or try to be flexible and make the change.

- Engage students in activities that focus on recognizing and understanding emotions. Books, games, or activities that help students identify and express their feelings promote emotional flexibility, which can in turn lead to cognitive flexibility. When students can understand and control their emotions, they are less anxious, and low levels of anxiety enable them to look at situations clearly and make changes accordingly.
- Encourage perspective-taking skills through exercises and read-alouds that prompt students to consider different viewpoints. For example, you can tell the story of The Three Little Pigs and then read *The True Story of the Three Little Pigs* (Scieszka, 2014) to show how different the story looks from the point of view of the wolf. You can continue to explore various perspectives as you read other stories and historical accounts and discuss famous artists and other major figures. You can also pull from events from students' own

lives, if they're open to it. Whether you're discussing the feelings of characters or real people, you're fostering empathy, which relies on and builds emotional and cognitive flexibility.
- Play executive function games that challenge working memory and cognitive flexibility, like memory games, puzzles, pattern recognition games, and strategy games. Any games that require decision making or problem solving, switching between different concepts, or adapting to new rules or patterns are especially helpful for building cognitive flexibility.
- Reinforce a growth mindset by praising students' effort, perseverance, and adaptability.
- Collaborate with parents and caregivers to reinforce cognitive flexibility strategies to ensure comprehensive support.

Strategies for Older Students

Cognitive flexibility strategies for older students build on their developing cognitive abilities and help them navigate more complex academic and social situations. Middle and high school students must learn to juggle assignments and deadlines, balance schoolwork and extracurriculars, adjust to new school rules, adapt writing styles to assignments in different classes, learn to use new technology, and navigate social situations like peer pressure and new relationships. Here are strategies for improving cognitive flexibility in older students:

- Encourage project- or problem-based learning, which requires students to hone their cognitive flexibility by exploring topics from different angles, developing creative solutions to problems, often working collaboratively, and thinking independently (Larmer, 2015; Yucel et al., 2016).
- Facilitate debates and discussions on topics that require students to articulate different viewpoints.
- Create opportunities for interdisciplinary learning to show how concepts from different subjects are interconnected, helping students see the relevance and application of knowledge across diverse domains. This process could be as complex as planning units with your grade-level or content-area team or as simple as the following classroom example. When I was teaching ELA to 6th graders,

I tried having them exchange and grade one another's assessments. Because there were 40 items on the assessment, the students needed to take 2.5 points off for each incorrect answer and then multiply 2.5 by the correct number of items. They all looked at me as though they had never multiplied with decimals before. Some even said, "You never taught us how to do this!" Having taught 6th grade math the previous year, I knew they had covered this and reminded the students that they indeed had this skill. This exercise was an opportunity to show the students that what they learned in one class could be used in another content area—and a great way to overcome cognitive inflexibility!

- Incorporate flexible grouping strategies so that students are exposed to different working styles and perspectives. Rotate group assignments to promote collaboration with a variety of classmates. Students who become anxious or rigid when assigned to a new group may benefit from having a home group that they know they'll return to.
- Design critical thinking exercises that challenge students to evaluate information from various sources, question assumptions, and identify biases.
- Group students into teams and present them with a hypothetical challenge to solve (e.g., "You're stranded on a desert island. What do you do to try and survive?").
- Take turns telling a story about a picture (of an object, a person or an animal, a place, a scene—there's really no limit). You can begin, then pass the picture to the next person, who continues the story. Each student must incorporate the information already stated while improvising the next part of the story.
- Play a game called "This Is Not" by passing around an everyday object and thinking of what else it could be. For example, you could start by holding up a pencil and saying, "This is not a pencil, it's a rolling pin." The next person might say, "This is not a rolling pin, it's a baseball bat." And so on.
- Use brainstorming sessions, mind mapping, or creative writing prompts to promote flexible thinking. For instance, give students writing prompts that require them to continue a story from different points of view or change the ending.

- Challenge students to play games differently. They can rewrite the directions to create a new game or just mix up the directions.
- Change your routine or change the environment. For example, remove the chairs from students' desks and see how they will react. Let them come up with a solution to the problem of not having chairs. Or give students their homework assignment at the beginning of class and save the opening activity until the end. Ask students what they think would change the routine and how they might feel about it.
- Incorporate reflective journaling to encourage students to think critically about their own thought processes. Prompt them to analyze situations, consider alternative approaches, and reflect on their decision making. You may even have them create sections for each of the executive functions and encourage them to reflect on their skills.
- Bring in guest speakers or experts from various fields to expose students to diverse perspectives and career paths.
- Present students with ethical dilemmas to discuss. Here's one example I've used myself: "Emily was not invited to a party that her best friend, Emma, was invited to. Emma attended the party but insisted that she not be in any photos that might be placed on social media. She avoided all but one candid shot. How might Emily feel seeing Emma at the party? Should Emma have told Emily that she was attending? Why or why not?"
- Integrate technology in your classroom that allows students to explore information in different formats. Encourage students to use multimedia sources to broaden their understanding of topics.
- Engage students in experiential learning, such as through science experiments and field trips, that might cause them to change their points of view about a topic. Real-world experiences like service-learning projects and internships are especially helpful in developing cognitive flexibility.
- Guide students in self-reflection and goal-setting activities. Have them assess their strengths and areas for growth related to cognitive flexibility.

These strategies are designed to challenge and stretch students' thinking, fostering cognitive flexibility as they navigate the complexities of academic and real-world situations. It's essential to create an environment that values open-mindedness, encourages curiosity, and supports students in developing the skills needed to adapt to diverse challenges.

Conclusion

Cognitive flexibility is a lifelong and potentially life-saving skill. Social-emotional learning skills can help strengthen this crucial skill, as students learn how to recognize their feelings and manage their emotions and reactions. When flexibility is called for—as when routines or schedules change—resistant students need to examine their reactions, understand them, and be able to adapt to meet shifting needs and expectations.

6

Self-Monitoring

Cathy entered the room like a tornado, destroying everything she came into contact with. It didn't matter that students were working quietly at their desks or that the teacher put her index finger up to her lips to indicate silence. Nothing mattered except what Cathy needed. After slamming the door, she tripped over the trash can, making a loud noise, and instead of apologizing or even moving the can back to the corner, she strode into the room and loudly addressed the class: "I can't find my colored pencils or any construction paper for my project. Who's taking all the construction paper? Where are my pencils? Can people help me find them? It's really important!"

Not only does Cathy lack the ability to adapt her behavior to her surroundings, but she also doesn't realize or care how her behavior affects others. Cathy has few friends, as many think she is full of herself and insensitive to others' feelings. For her part, she blames everyone else for her failures.

Though Cathy may lack self-control and be self-centered, first and foremost, she has very weak self-monitoring skills. According to Searle (2013), "learning how to accurately assess their own performance and use this information to make adjustments goes a long way toward building all the executive skills" (p. 18). Cathy needs to learn to take social, verbal, and setting cues into consideration to ascertain if a behavior change is necessary.

The definition of self-monitoring I find most helpful is from school and clinical psychologist Marie-Josée Gendron (n.d.): "Self-monitoring is the ability to evaluate our own behavior in order to determine when a different approach would be more appropriate. So it's about noticing and fixing our mistakes, knowing when to ask for help. In a learning environment, a student with good self-monitoring will reread his work, make sure he does the checks and balances to make sure that their answers make sense. The student who is challenged with self-monitoring will not engage in such tasks, and of course the quality of their work will suffer."

Put simply, self-monitoring involves observing, evaluating, and regulating our thoughts, behaviors, and actions. It is a vital component of the broader executive function skill set and is closely linked to metacognition. Following are some key aspects of self-monitoring:

- Students engage in self-observation by noticing and cultivating awareness of their thoughts and behaviors in real time.
- Following observation, students evaluate their thoughts and behaviors, considering whether they align to goals, standards, or expectations.
- If necessary, evaluation leads to modification of thoughts or behaviors. In this respect, self-monitoring is closely tied to cognitive flexibility.
- Students identify obstacles and devise strategies to surmount them in real time.
- Students track progress toward goals.

Self-monitoring plays a role in such tasks as planning, organizing, managing time, and regulating emotions. Students use self-monitoring to assess their understanding of material, identify areas of difficulty, and adjust their study strategies. In social interactions, they use self-monitoring to assess the impact of their words and actions on others, adjusting their behavior to maintain positive relationships. Educators and parents can support the development of self-monitoring skills by providing opportunities for reflection, encouraging goal setting, and teaching strategies for problem solving and adaptability.

What the Research Says

Self-monitoring skills develop gradually across childhood and adolescence, growing and changing as the prefrontal cortex matures. Ori Brafman (2011) of Stanford University refers to those who know how to observe their own behavior and adjust it in all situations as "self-monitors." According to Brafman, self-monitoring or lack of it can have a substantial impact on our brain chemistry. Students who do not self-monitor can become stressed out when their lack of attention has repercussions they don't expect (such as receiving poor grades). Stress releases cortisol in the brain and restricts access to working memory, making learning and understanding more difficult. By contrast, students with strong self-monitoring skills who actively review the environment, read the emotions of others, and make changes in behaviors release "good" chemicals: oxytocin as trust and friendships are gained, dopamine as goals are set and met, and serotonin as a reward for success.

Research on self-monitoring skills highlights the importance of strategies that foster metacognition, including self-reflection and self-questioning. Students who are explicitly taught to monitor their understanding and adjust their learning strategies have been shown to excel academically (Guo, 2022). Timely and constructive feedback encourages self-monitoring, too, as it helps students assess their performance, identify areas for improvement, and make any necessary adjustments.

It's important to note that the effectiveness of interventions may vary based on individual characteristics, and a combination of strategies may be most beneficial. In addition, ongoing research continues to explore innovative approaches to developing self-monitoring skills, particularly in the context of cognitive and metacognitive interventions for diverse populations.

Self-monitoring skills develop gradually in the brain through early adulthood. The general timeline of development is as follows:

- **Early childhood (3–5 years).** Basic self-monitoring emerges, including in the form of self-talk. Children begin to observe and imitate the behaviors of those around them and develop an initial awareness of their own actions and the actions of others.
- **Middle childhood (6–12 years).** Children start to develop a greater awareness of their own thoughts and emotions and are increasingly

able to reflect on their behavior and understand basic cause-and-effect relationships.
- **Adolescence (13–18 years).** Self-awareness and reflection skills continue to develop, and the ability to adjust behavior to conform with both internal standards and societal expectations evolves.
- **Early adulthood (18–25 years).** Young adults become more adept at evaluating their own performance, setting goals, and adjusting their behavior to meet those goals. They are increasingly able to reflect on long-term consequences and make decisions accordingly.

Factors that contribute to the development of self-monitoring skills include

- The pace of maturation of the prefrontal cortex throughout childhood and adolescence;
- Social interactions and experiences that underscore the importance of societal norms and expectations;
- Educational opportunities, strategies, and interventions; and
- Cultural norms and values.

The SEL Connection

Figure 6.1 shows the connections between SEL skills and self-monitoring. Integrating self-monitoring into SEL programs and educational practices

- Helps individuals develop a strong foundation for social and emotional well-being;
- Promotes self-reflection, adaptive behaviors, and a heightened awareness of one's own emotions and actions across social contexts; and
- Contributes to the creation of a supportive and emotionally intelligent learning environment.

Characteristics of Underdeveloped Self-Monitoring in Students

Following are some common signs of self-monitoring difficulties in students:

Figure 6.1. The SEL Connection to Self-Monitoring

SEL Skill	Connection to Self-Monitoring
Self-Awareness	Self-awareness is foundational for self-monitoring. It helps students recognize when their behavior or emotions are not aligned with their goals or expectations, enabling them to make necessary adjustments. This process involves understanding internal states and recognizing how those states influence actions and outcomes.
Self-Management	Effective self-management includes the ability to monitor and control impulses, sustain attention, and stay on task. These skills help students to regularly check their performance and behavior against their goals, making real-time adjustments to improve outcomes.
Social Awareness	Social awareness helps students to monitor and adjust their behavior in social contexts. By understanding how their actions affect others, students can modify their behavior to foster positive interactions and relationships.
Relationship Skills	Relationship skills enable students to effectively navigate social interactions, including being aware of and responding to social cues, which requires constant self-monitoring to ensure appropriate behavior and effective communication.
Responsible Decision Making	Making responsible decisions involves evaluating the consequences of various actions and making adjustments based on those evaluations. Self-monitoring is crucial in this process, as it allows students to reflect on their choices and outcomes and adjust their behavior accordingly.

- **Lack of awareness of mistakes.** Students may be unable to recognize when they've made errors, whether in their schoolwork or in life outside the classroom.
- **Inconsistent performance.** Students may perform well on some assignments but poorly on others or over time.
- **Difficulty following instructions.** Students may misunderstand or misinterpret instructions, leading to incomplete or inaccurate work.
- **Impulsivity.** Students may struggle to regulate impulsive responses.
- **Poor time management.** Students may underestimate the time required for tasks, leading to rushed, late, or incomplete work. Outside the classroom, students may struggle to effectively manage time around daily routines or plan for activities.

- **Limited goal setting.** Students may have difficulty breaking larger assignments down into manageable steps.
- **Inattention to detail.** Students may struggle to thoroughly review and edit their assignments for accuracy.
- **Difficulty with organization.** Students may have messy desks, struggle with keeping track of assignments, and misplace important materials.
- **Lack of reflection on learning.** Students may have difficulty or be unaccustomed to reflecting on their strengths, weaknesses, and areas for improvement.
- **Social challenges.** Students may struggle to recognize social cues, leading to difficulty forming and maintaining positive relationships.

Recognizing the signs and providing targeted support and interventions can contribute to the social and academic success of your students with self-monitoring difficulties. In addition, you may wish to use the Self-Monitoring Self-Assessment in Figure 6.2.

Strategies for Younger Students

Teaching young students to self-monitor begins with ensuring students have a clear understanding of what the process looks like. Self-monitoring provides students with more immediate feedback than you can provide. Following are some strategies for improving self-monitoring skills in younger students:

- Ensure that students keep track of what they are doing and how they are thinking so they can adjust their behaviors and thoughts to meet goals or complete tasks (Porter, 2002; Smith, 2002).
- Point out when you see proper monitoring behavior and when you don't. Leave a sticky note on students' desks to applaud their behavior or learning. High school teacher Ms. Reid leaves notes that say, "I like the data I am collecting on your self-monitoring!" If she doesn't see what she wants to see, she speaks to students in person: "Right now, I'm not observing strong self-monitoring. What can I do to help?"
- Have students use checklists of common self-monitoring mistakes and have them check for them on a daily or weekly basis.

Figure 6.2. Self-Monitoring Self-Assessment

Put a check mark in the column that best describes you in these learning situations.	Always	Often	Sometimes	Rarely	Never
I complete my projects at the last minute because I don't keep track of time.					
I never know when it's a test day because I don't remember the dates my teacher gives us.					
When I work a math problem, I don't check over my work, so I don't always have the best answer.					
I can't get organized enough to have time to study and see my friends.					
When I study for a test, I tend to rush through or skip my notes and class papers.					
When I make a mistake on a problem, instead of going over it to see what I did wrong, I just skip it.					
I do not have a designated place to study.					
I am never ready for a pop quiz because I don't study my notes.					
I lack strategies to help me understand new concepts, like drawing pictures or maps.					
I never seem to have enough time to get my homework done because there are too many subjects.					

- Model asking the questions you want students to ask themselves (e.g., "Does that look right to you?" "Did you show your work?" "Why are you reading this story?").
- Explicitly teach self-monitoring skills to students in the context of the content areas (e.g., rechecking answers in math systematically, rereading and checking grammar and spelling in writing tasks for English).

- Help students recognize when they need a break and establish a signal for them to ask for one.
- Implement flexible seating. Some students learn best at a desk, others at a table, still others on the floor. The more comfortable they are, the better able they are to monitor their behavior.
- Give students classroom jobs. Holding the book as you read, making a list on the board as you discuss, and handing out materials all help keep kids aware of what is going on.
- Be sure your lessons aren't too long. Keep attention spans in mind as you prepare lessons and units. You may also break your longer lessons into chunks. It's easier to self-monitor for shorter periods of time.
- Create cue cards with simple visuals and reminders for expected behaviors. Encourage students to use the cards to self-monitor and to check their behavior against the expectations.
- Have students play musical instruments where possible, as doing so can help develop both selective attention and self-monitoring skills. Research suggests that the practice of two-handed coordination supports better executive function (Center on the Developing Child at Harvard University, 2014).
- Institute a "traffic lights" system. This is a great way to get feedback immediately on a newer topic. I give students a red, green, and yellow card. At any time during a lesson I will ask, "Are you understanding this?" Green is for yes, red is for no, and yellow is for not sure or maybe. This practice forces students to monitor where they are in the learning while also helping you to figure out next steps.
- Use "emotion cards" with pictures or emojis on them representing different emotions. To promote self-awareness and self-monitoring, encourage students to select and share cards that reflect their emotional states. You can have them put the card on their desks and then walk around to monitor how they're feeling.
- Implement a buddy system so students can support one another's self-monitoring. Buddies can check in on each other's progress and offer encouragement using a checklist like the one in Figure 6.3.

Consistency is key when implementing these strategies. By creating a classroom culture that values self-awareness and self-regulation,

Figure 6.3. Buddy System Checklist for Self-Monitoring

My buddy's name is _____.

My name is _____.

Put a check mark next to each statement that was true for the day. Add up the check marks at the end and put the number next to your buddy's name at the bottom.

	My buddy had everything they needed.
	My buddy understood everything they had to do.
	When my buddy needed help, they asked for it.
	My buddy followed the directions.
	My buddy was on task today.
	My buddy stayed calm today.
	My buddy recognized their mistakes and fixed them.
	My buddy got their work done.
	My buddy listened to feedback and used it to improve.
	My buddy only needed one reminder to stay on task today.

My buddy got _____ check marks today.

teachers can contribute to the development of strong self-monitoring skills in younger students. Additionally, involving parents and caregivers in reinforcing these strategies at home can enhance their effectiveness.

Strategies for Older Students

Improving self-monitoring skills in older students is about leveraging their existing cognitive abilities while fostering autonomy and responsibility. Here are some strategies for improving self-monitoring in older students:

- Implement interventions focused on identifying and changing thought patterns and behaviors.
- Encourage students to use apps and tools that provide real-time feedback, prompts for reflection, and goal-tracking features.
- Provide clear instructions, model self-monitoring behaviors, and guide students through the process of monitoring and adjusting their learning.

- Tailor scaffolds to students' individual needs. Some learners may require more initial support before developing independent self-monitoring skills.
- Connect self-monitoring skills to real-world tasks and contexts.
- Have students use sticky notes to ask and answer questions while they are reading as a way to check in with themselves. Questions and fill-in statements like the following can be useful:
  – What have I read thus far?
  – At this point in the reading, do I understand the text?
  – What I find confusing so far is _____.
  – This reminds me of _____.
  – What new information have I read?
  – What do I think will be on the test?

  To get students started, provide sticky notes and have each student answer the prompts out loud.
- Provide students with a self-check sheet like the one in Figure 6.4 for recently completed assignments. Use this sheet as needed for students who need to strengthen their self-monitoring skills.
- Show students how to set specific, measurable, and achievable goals for academic tasks. Equip them with tools like goal-setting worksheets and digital apps for effective progress tracking.
- Have students use reflection journals or blogs to routinely articulate their learning experiences. Encourage them to reflect on strengths, areas for improvement, and successful strategies they've used.
- Utilize rubrics with self-assessment components for assignments and projects. Empower students to critically evaluate their work against established criteria and set improvement goals. Offer sample papers against which they can compare their work, and attach a copy of each rubric to their paper or writing prompt.
- Facilitate Socratic seminars or discussions where students take turns expressing their viewpoints. Encourage self-monitoring by asking students to reflect on their contributions and participation.
- Emphasize the importance of seeking feedback from peers and teachers on assignments. Peer assessment helps both students: The assessor gets a greater understanding of the content, and the student getting assessed gets information to work with.

Figure 6.4. Sample Self-Monitoring Checklist

Task	How Did I Do?	What Have I Learned?	How Will I Improve?
Civil War history paper	B-. I did OK, but I want to do better.	I need to write a longer paper with more research references.	I have to go beyond what's in the text. Do some research on the internet.
math test	80%	I didn't study much, and I could have worked with a study group.	I will make time to study more and join a study group if it's offered.
English essay	I turned my paper in late. I got a 50% for that.	I need to get my work in on time.	If I see that I'm not able to get my paper in, I will ask for an extension.

- Incorporate project-based learning activities that require students to plan, execute, and reflect on their work. Provide opportunities for self-assessment and peer feedback during project presentations.
- Conduct debriefing sessions after assessments or major assignments. These can be eye-opening for students. Discuss strategies that students used, what worked well, and areas where adjustments could be made.
- Similar to the buddy system for younger students, implement an accountability partner system where students pair up to support each other. Partners can discuss goals, check in on progress, and provide constructive feedback.
- Conduct individual conferences with students to discuss their academic progress, goals, and challenges. Provide personalized feedback and guidance for improvement.
- Celebrate both small and significant achievements to reinforce positive self-monitoring behaviors. Recognize and commend students for their effort, progress, and resilience.

By incorporating these strategies, educators can empower older students to take ownership of their learning, develop effective self-monitoring habits, and prepare for future academic and personal challenges. Creating an environment that values reflection, goal setting, and continuous improvement contributes to the development of responsible and self-aware learners.

The development of self-monitoring is not a linear process. Some students may demonstrate advanced self-monitoring skills at an earlier age, while others may require more time and support. In addition, the ongoing refinement of self-monitoring skills is influenced by experiences, feedback, and the application of these skills in various real-world contexts. Classroom environments that provide opportunities for reflection, goal setting, and learning from experiences contribute to students' continued development of self-monitoring skills throughout their lives.

Conclusion

Self-monitoring is a giant leap toward metacognition. Every time a student stops to assess what they are learning, evaluates progress on a task, or checks their goals, they exhibit the traits of metacognition. As they adjust their goals, realign their path to progress, and even just wonder about what they are learning, they are thinking about their thinking and their behavior. As a bonus, they are exercising cognitive flexibility to make those changes, are accessing working memory to assess their progress, and are deep in self-awareness and self-management.

Planning, Organization, Prioritization, and Time Management

Finding 14 algebra assignments that were completed but never turned in was a shock to both of Morgan's parents. Was it any wonder that her grades were not as they had hoped? When they sat down with her homeroom teacher and asked about her other content areas, they discovered her system for organization: the "pile" system. Picture in your mind piles of work that may or may not be neatly stacked atop a desk or messily heaped in a locker. At least they knew she was truthful when she told them her homework was *done*. Like many teens, she "organized" her room in much the same way: clean clothes were piled on her desk chair, and dirty clothes were piled—well, everywhere!

The reason for grouping the skills of planning, organization, prioritization, and time management together is that they often complement and support one another. For example, effective planning requires a clear understanding of priorities and the ability to allocate time appropriately (prioritization and time management); likewise, organization is essential for implementing plans and keeping track of tasks, deadlines, and resources. Here is a brief overview of these four executive function skills:

- **Planning** involves creating a roadmap to achieve a specific goal that identifies the steps, resources, and timelines necessary for doing so. To plan effectively, students should break tasks down into manageable steps, establish a sequence of actions, and consider potential obstacles or challenges.
- **Organization** refers to the arrangement and structuring of information, materials, or tasks in a systematic and orderly manner. To organize effectively, students should categorize information for optimal access and maintain a tidy and structured physical or digital environment.
- **Prioritization** involves determining the relative importance of tasks or goals and allocating time and resources accordingly. Students should assess tasks based on urgency and importance, make decisions about the order of completion, and avoid procrastination.
- **Time management** is the ability to use time efficiently and effectively to accomplish tasks. Students should set realistic deadlines, create schedules or routines, avoid time-wasting activities, and adapt plans when unexpected events occur.

Students with well-developed planning and organization EFS are better equipped to manage their responsibilities, complete tasks efficiently, and navigate complex situations. These skills are foundational for academic success, professional achievement, and overall effective daily functioning.

What the Research Says

According to a study by Best and Miller (2010), planning can have a substantial impact on academic outcomes. A paper by Friedman and Miyake (2017) explored the unity and diversity of executive functions, shedding light on how organizational skills contribute to cognitive processes. They noted that although executive functions like organizational skills are separate from other EFS, they all work together to create a general pattern of distinct actions that are similar among multiple ages and populations. Research by Dabbagh and Kitsantas (2012) discusses the role of time management and how it affects academic achievement in both formal and informal learning. They found that whether learning took place in the classroom or virtually, the ability to manage time efficiently led to better achievement overall. Similarly, Trentepohl and colleagues (2022) found that students who allocate time wisely for studying, assignments, and exams often experience better outcomes. Duckworth and colleagues (2007) highlight the importance of prioritizing in their discussion of grit and academic achievement. Effective time management and prioritizing have also been linked to lower stress levels (Aeon et al., 2021), higher grades (Evans et al., 2021), and overall life success (Hanover Research, 2016). In addition, studies indicate that individuals with strong planning skills are often better equipped to adapt to changing circumstances and demonstrate increased cognitive flexibility (Friedman & Robbins, 2022).

Neuroimaging studies suggest that the dorsolateral prefrontal cortex is heavily involved in planning and organization processes (Pochon et al., 2001) and that these processes contribute to better memory performance and social functioning (Sippl, 2020). Difficulty with these processes is associated with mental health conditions such as depression and anxiety.

A general timeline of development of these executive function skills is as follows:

- **Early childhood (3–5 years).** Children might begin planning their play or organizing their toys in a particular manner.
- **Middle childhood (6–12 years).** Children start to organize their belongings and prioritize tasks, like homework versus play.
- **Adolescence (13–18 years).** Students plan for longer-term projects and goals. They begin developing a better sense of time and can manage it more effectively for tasks. They can consider multiple strategies to solve a problem and choose the best one.
- **Early adulthood (18–25 years).** As the prefrontal cortex reaches maturity, young adults are able to prioritize their time and use helpful tools for planning and organization. If they are in the workforce or living on their own, they use all the EF skills for getting

work done, budgeting their money, and balancing their work and social life.

The SEL Connection

Figure 7.1 shows the connection between SEL skills and the executive functions of planning, organization, prioritization, and time management. The connection between social-emotional learning and these four EFS is integral to students' holistic development, emotional well-being, interpersonal relationships, and academic success.

Figure 7.1. The SEL Connection to Planning, Organization, Prioritization, and Time Management

SEL Skill	Connection to Planning, Organization, Prioritization, and Time Management
Self-Awareness	Self-awareness enables students to understand their own strengths and weaknesses and thereby set realistic goals and create effective plans, understand their personal organization styles and preferences, recognize what is important to them based on their personal values and needs, and know how their energy levels and moods affect their productivity, which can help them manage time effectively.
Self-Management	Self-management helps students develop strategies, structure their tasks and environment, set priorities, and allocate time to manage their workload and attain their goals.
Social Awareness	Social awareness supports students' ability to consider the effect of their actions on others when making plans, to work collaboratively to organize group tasks and responsibilities, to balance personal goals with the needs and expectations of others, and to coordinate schedules and deadlines in group activities.
Relationship Skills	Relationship skills help students plan for effective communication and conflict resolution, organize social events and collaboration, prioritize relationships and social interactions, and manage time to maintain relationships and social connections.
Responsible Decision Making	Responsible decision making supports students in their efforts to weigh options and consider consequences when they make decisions, structure decisions in a logical and organized manner, make decisions based on ethical considerations and prioritizing long-term benefits, and decide how to allocate time and resources effectively.

Characteristics of Underdeveloped Planning, Organization, Prioritization, and Time Management Skills in Students

Following are some common signs of underdeveloped planning, organization, prioritization, and time management skills:

- **Disorganization.** Students are disorganized, misplace assignments, and have difficulty keeping track of materials.
- **Time management.** Students return assignments late if at all (sometimes due to the inability to find the assignments—see "disorganization"). Students may have difficulty estimating the amount of time required to complete tasks, and they may delay working on assignments until the last minute. These issues may result in incomplete or rushed work.
- **Inconsistent work quality.** Quality of work can vary as students struggle with deadlines.
- **Inability to set priorities.** Students have trouble with decision making and may spend an inordinate amount of time on less critical issues, missing the forest for the trees.
- **Lack of planning.** Students have difficulty planning and organizing both short- and long-term projects and assignments.
- **Forgetfulness.** Students may forget materials and important dates.
- **Poor task initiation.** Students may be unable to start tasks without being reminded to do so.
- **Tardiness.** Students may frequently arrive late to class, scheduled activities, or social events.
- **Relationship strain.** Students may encounter strain in both school and personal relationships due to difficulty planning and organizing around shared commitments.

Recognizing these characteristics in students as early as possible allows for targeted interventions. Remember as well that students' executive function skills develop differently, and strengths may vary based on individual factors. Consider using the self-assessment in Figure 7.2

Figure 7.2. Planning, Organization, Prioritization, and Time Management Self-Assessment

Put a check mark in the column that best describes you in these learning situations.	Always	Often	Sometimes	Rarely	Never
I don't have a dedicated space for doing homework; I work on it anywhere I can.					
I don't bother (or I forget) to write down my assignments.					
I don't come to class prepared with the necessary materials and have to borrow them from classmates or the teacher.					
I have trouble finishing my homework.					
I don't finish long-term projects because I don't know where to start.					
I procrastinate on homework and/or stay up late to finish it, so I'm tired at school.					
I don't plan out work and free time. I play first and see if there's time afterward to do schoolwork.					
When I have multiple tasks, I can't figure out which is most important or time-sensitive, so sometimes I don't do anything.					
I turn in my work whenever it gets done, so it tends to be late.					
My materials are scattered and disorganized both at home and at school.					

to help students assess their competency with planning, organization, prioritization, and time management.

Strategies for Younger Students

Following are some classroom strategies to enhance planning, organization, prioritization, and time management in younger students:

- Before starting a project, help students identify the steps they should take and write them down in a planner.
- Take the time to help students organize their notebooks. This will save time, frustration, and energy in the long run.
- Use think-alouds to model the steps for assignments. Ask students to share with the class or small group what they would do. It can also be helpful for students who are especially good at certain tasks, such as studying for tests, to share their planning and organizing strategies.
- Have students keep and frequently consult a list of academic goals.
- Ensure that students keep track of their homework in a planner.
- Divide big projects into chunks and create a due date for each chunk.
- Estimate how long each assignment may take and work with your students to prioritize the component tasks.
- For students who are just starting to learn how to plan, use a simple plan sheet that is folded in half. Have them label the left side *Today* and the right side *Tomorrow*. Under *Today*, students write down what they will be doing the rest of the day; under *Tomorrow*, they list what they know they will be doing tomorrow. This is good practice for eventually filling out weekly or monthly planners.

These strategies are designed to scaffold and support the development of planning and organization skills in younger students. Consistency, modeling, and a positive and supportive classroom environment are key factors in helping students build these essential executive function skills.

Strategies for Older Students

Building and refining planning and organization skills is crucial for older students' academic success and personal development. Here are classroom strategies specifically tailored for older students:

- Emphasize the concept of deadlines and help students understand the consequences of not meeting them. Have students practice estimating the amount of time an assignment might take, writing down that time, and comparing their estimate with the actual time taken. For big group projects, assign project managers whose main responsibility is to coordinate time for each step of the project and the role of each team member. Planning and prioritizing multiple assignments and projects will provide practice for now and the future. Remind students that they already prioritize activities that are important to them, like getting to football practice or their weekend job on time, and as adults they will need to prioritize what may be more important to others.

- Encourage students to use calendars or planners to plan and schedule their tasks.
- Model organization in the classroom, such as by ensuring there's a clearly labeled box for turning in homework. Keep materials in designated areas and color-code files.
- Use or encourage students to use time-management aids such as timers or alarms.
- Have students set specific, measurable, achievable, relevant, and time-bound (SMART) goals by asking the following questions:
  – **Specific:** What do I want to accomplish? Who or what do I need to reach this goal? What are the requirements?
  – **Measurable:** How will I measure my achievement of the goal? What data will I collect?
  – **Achievable:** Is the goal doable? Do I have the necessary skills and resources? What else might I need to achieve this goal?
  – **Relevant:** How does the goal align with broader goals? Why is meeting the goal important? How might it help me in the future?
  – **Time-bound:** What is the time frame for accomplishing the goal? Is it possible for me to meet the goal in this time frame?

It's important to explain to students that writing down goals makes it more likely to achieve them. Neuroscientists have found that people who picture or describe their goals very vividly are anywhere from 1.2 to 1.4 times more likely to successfully accomplish them (Murphy, 2018).

These strategies are designed to empower older students with the planning and organization skills they need to navigate the increasing complexity of their academic and personal responsibilities. Encouraging self-directed learning and fostering a growth mindset can further support their development of these essential executive function skills.

Conclusion

It's important to be flexible and patient when teaching students planning, organization, prioritization, and time management skills—the interlocking executive function skills that are essential for academic achievement and real-world success. Students' brains are changing rapidly, and just when you think they've "got it," you can be sorely disappointed. Celebrate student successes and provide positive reinforcement whenever possible.

8

SEL and EFS: Fulfilling the Dream

> There comes a point where we need to stop just pulling people out of the river. We need to go upstream and find out why they're falling in.
>
> —Bishop Desmond Tutu

We probably all have known students over the years who we knew were perfectly capable learners yet did not seem to function well in the classroom. We may have even gone so far as to remove them from the classroom or learning group because they interrupted others' ability to learn. As Oprah Winfrey quoted the words of her friend and mentor Maya Angelou, "You did what you knew how to do, and when you knew better, you did better" (OWN, 2011)—and it's time for *us* to do better, for the sake of *all* our students.

In addition to promoting social connectedness, social-emotional learning encourages brain development by helping to shape the brain's neural circuitry and, ultimately, our executive function skills, which are crucial for success in the 21st century.

As you have seen in this book, social-emotional skills and executive function skills are interdependent. For example, social awareness, an SEL competency, allows students to identify their emotions, and impulse inhibition, an EFS, permits them to control those emotions. Both sets of skills are controlled by the same area of the brain, the prefrontal cortex—which is why neuroscientists like Bruce Perry (2023) tell us to focus on developing that region. We want to shift students as much as possible from a lower survival or emotional state to a higher-level executive state, and SEL tools are among the most effective ways to do so. And rather than punish behaviors or provide consequences for students who have difficulty making this shift, we need to help them prevent those behaviors in the first place (Desautels, 2024).

Transformative SEL

CASEL (n.d.) describes transformative SEL as "a form of SEL implementation where young people and adults build strong, respectful, and lasting relationships to engage in co-learning. It facilitates critical examination of individual and contextual factors that contribute to inequities and collaborative solutions that lead to personal, community, and societal well-being." It is about helping students realize their potential, developing partnerships with them, supporting their strengths and ambitions, and helping to close gaps in opportunities and outcomes. According to Jagers and colleagues (2021), transformative SEL "concentrates SEL practice on transforming inequitable settings and systems and promoting justice-oriented civic engagement" (para. 9).

Transformative SEL emphasizes the importance of identity, agency, belonging, collaborative problem solving, and curiosity to students' development:

- A sense of *identity* serves as a buffer against negative experiences.
- A sense of *agency* ensures that students expect to have a voice in their futures.

- A sense of *belonging* is vital to ensuring that students feel that others accept them and care about them.
- *Collaborative problem solving* allows students to develop common understandings and devise solutions by merging knowledge and skills.
- *Curiosity* is fundamental to the pursuit of knowledge and to understanding different points of view.

Transformative SEL is concerned with developing the whole child in school—not just their academic achievement, but the health of their brains and bodies as well. This development is especially important for students who have faced trauma, which we know lives in the brain *and* the body—meaning that the sense of threat and helplessness resulting from that trauma negatively affects the functions of students' bodies as well as their brains (van der Kolk, 2015). Transformative SEL recognizes the importance of nurturing students' emotional intelligence, interpersonal skills, and ability to make ethical decisions. It calls for equity and inclusion in every learning environment and values diversity of experiences and perspectives. The overarching goal is to prepare students for challenges and help them learn to bounce back from setbacks—both of which rely on well-developed executive function skills.

The Intersection of Executive Function and Social-Emotional Learning

As we've explored throughout this book, executive functions play a crucial role in weaving SEL into academics by providing the cognitive processes necessary for effective self-regulation, goal-setting, and adaptive behaviors. Let's review some of these EF-SEL intersections:

- Impulse inhibition is a fundamental aspect of self-regulation and relationship skills, helping students manage their emotions and behaviors and foster positive relationships with peers and teachers.
- Working memory is essential for managing and regulating emotions. It allows students to hold and manipulate information about their emotional state and keep in mind how similar experiences worked out in the past, enabling them to make informed decisions about how to respond in social situations.

- Attention and focus support self-management and decision making and play a role in all SEL skills. They enable students to use the mental processes needed to examine their behavior as well as to engage in academics.
- Cognitive flexibility supports social awareness and relationship skills. Being able to adapt thinking and behaviors enables students to understand others' perspectives as well as navigate through unexpected changes and challenges.
- Self-monitoring supports self-reflection, enabling students to reflect on their learning experiences, identify strengths and areas for improvement, and adapt their strategies accordingly.
- The EF skills of planning, organization, prioritization, and time management intersect with SEL skills in numerous ways, including the following:
  - Planning and organization equip students to make more informed decisions about their learning and manage responsibilities effectively.
  - Prioritization involves responsible decision making. Students consider consequences for themselves and others related to the choices they make.
  - Improving their time management skills helps students handle stress and deadlines, enhancing their emotional well-being. Conversely, self-awareness and self-regulation help students become more aware of prioritization and time management as it relates to themselves and others.
  - Goal setting is a shared aspect of these four executive functions and SEL. When students set academic and personal goals, they are engaging in self-awareness and self-management. Achieving these goals strengthens motivation and a positive mindset.

By emphasizing executive functions within academic contexts, educators can create environments that naturally incorporate SEL principles. Explicitly teaching and reinforcing these executive skills can enhance students' ability to navigate the academic and social dimensions of their learning journey. This integration contributes to the development of well-rounded individuals with both cognitive and social-emotional competence.

Schoolwide SEL Includes EFS

Schoolwide SEL is a holistic approach to fostering students' social-emotional development across various domains, and integrating EFS alongside SEL initiatives enhances their effectiveness of these programs. Here's how schoolwide processes can further both SEL skills and EFS at the same time:

- **Explicit instruction.** SEL programs include explicit instruction on core SEL competencies, and educators can ensure the same for EF skills as part of SEL curriculum. This helps students develop cognitive skills that support their emotional well-being and interpersonal relationships.
- **Curriculum alignment.** Just as SEL initiatives can be embedded in the academic curriculum, so too can EFS. For example, problem solving can emphasize cognitive flexibility, task completion can incorporate organization, and all subjects can emphasize working memory.
- **Professional development.** Schoolwide SEL often involves providing professional development for educators, which can also be provided for recognizing and addressing executive function challenges in students and lead to more supportive learning environments.
- **Assessment and monitoring.** Schools use assessments to monitor students' SEL competencies and inform targeted interventions. Assessments can also include measures of EFS, providing insights into individual students' cognitive strengths and areas for improvement to guide personalized support.
- **Inclusive practices.** Like SEL initiatives, EFS development promotes a sense of belonging and acceptance for all students. Recognizing and accommodating diverse executive function profiles contributes to creating an inclusive environment that supports students with varying cognitive strengths and challenges.
- **Behavioral interventions.** Schoolwide SEL often incorporates positive behavior interventions and support (PBIS) strategies to reinforce expected behaviors, which can also help students to develop their EFS.

- **Parent and community involvement.** Involving parents and the community is a key element of schoolwide SEL, and the same should be true for EFS initiatives.
- **Environment and culture.** Schoolwide initiatives for both SEL and EFS aim to create a positive and supportive school culture.

By intentionally integrating executive functions into the fabric of schoolwide SEL initiatives, schools can create a comprehensive framework that addresses both the social-emotional and cognitive aspects of students' development.

Promoting EFS to Parents and Communities

Promoting EFS to parents and communities involves providing them with information, resources, and support to enhance understanding and collaboration. The concept of executive function skills may be new to some, so the best place to start is by raising awareness. Here are a few strategies you may wish to implement for this purpose:

- Organize workshops or training sessions for parents and community members focused on understanding EFS. Once these stakeholders learn more about these skills, they will be able to look for signs of underdevelopment in students.
- Integrate a short introduction to EFS into Back-to-School nights using some of the material in this book, and share strategies for parents to use at home to support students' skill development.
- Throughout the year, develop and distribute informative materials, brochures, or newsletters that explain the importance of executive functions and encourage collaborative goal setting among parents, teachers, and students.
- Post a list of EFS resources for parents online that include articles, videos, and webinars.
- Use parent-teacher conferences as an opportunity to discuss executive functions.
- Provide families with personalized insights into their child's EFS strengths and challenges and collaboratively develop strategies for

support. If using the self-assessments included in this book, share those so families understand what to look for.
- Use social media groups or messaging apps to share tips and resources on executive functions.
- Foster a sense of community by encouraging parents to share their successes and challenges.

Combining the Dreams of SEL and EFS Development

The integration of transformative SEL and EFS development predicts a groundbreaking educational standard that emphasizes the whole child. This vision involves preparing students not just for academic success but also for life beyond the classroom by equipping them with the necessary life skills. Both in school and outside it, students must know how to navigate complex situations, collaborate with others, and adapt to changing circumstances. Transformative SEL and EFS development alike advocate for a positive learning culture where students feel supported, engaged, and encouraged to take risks.

Empowering students with a sense of agency is a central theme in both transformative SEL and EFS development. Students should be active participants in their learning journey, capable of making informed decisions, solving intricate problems, and effectively managing their emotions while also maintaining inclusive and equitable educational environments, addressing diverse student needs, and valuing different learning approaches.

Both transformative SEL and an EFS-focused approach recognize the critical role of educators and emphasize the need for teacher professional development. Within these approaches, teachers are viewed as facilitators not only of academic knowledge but also of social-emotional and executive skill development. Continuous improvement and assessment are integral components of the shared vision, requiring regular evaluation of the effectiveness of SEL and executive function interventions, adaptive strategies based on feedback, and responsiveness to evolving educational needs. In such a model, teachers would have the necessary tools and training to create educational experiences that are comprehensive, inclusive, and empowering and create well-rounded individuals capable of navigating the complexities of the 21st century.

It Starts with the Adults

Consider using a short EFS self-assessment like the one in Figure 8.1 with educators and staff so that everyone is aware of their own strengths and needs. It may also help generate more interest in the EFS development process among the adults at school. Everyone could complete it just before or during a staff meeting, giving colleagues the opportunity to chat and share their own personal strengths and struggles. Choosing buddies who will check in on each other could be helpful in keeping

Figure 8.1. EFS Self-Assessment for Educators

Put a check mark in the column that best describes you in these learning situations.	Always	Often	Sometimes	Rarely	Never
If my first idea or strategy doesn't work, I give up.					
I have difficulty making a plan and following it.					
I avoid making long-term goals for myself.					
I focus on one thing at a time to the exclusion of all else.					
I have trouble figuring out how long a lesson will take to teach.					
When I have little time and lots to do, I am not great at prioritizing and sometimes freeze.					
I say things without thinking.					
I use the "pile" system, and my desk is a mess.					
I'm slow getting ready for work, and I am sometimes late for appointments.					
I tend to misplace my keys, phone, or sunglasses.					
I don't notice or care if my students' desks or workspaces are tidy.					

everyone focused on practicing and modeling good executive function skills.

The research is clear: SEL works (Aspen Institute, 2019; Cipriano et al., 2023) and teaching EFS works, too (Diamond & Lee, 2011; Zelazo & Carlson, 2020). Putting them together helps to doubly ensure students' success (Low, 2021). I have been saying for years that SEL is not so much about *what* you teach as about *how* you teach—and even more than that, it's who you are. Both SEL and EFS development can not only lead our students into a brighter future, but also give us as educators the sense of fulfillment we all are seeking.

Appendix A: Universal Executive Function Strategies

The strategies presented here have been shown to fortify executive function skills across the board in all classrooms for all students.

Role-Play

According to Stephanie Carlson at the Institute of Child Development and her colleagues (2014), role-playing helps students become more flexible and objective in their thinking. By pretending to be someone else, students feel a psychological distance between themselves and a given task that allows them to be calmer, more persistent, and more creative in completing it (White & Carlson, 2021).

Be sure to engage students in role-playing activities where they can practice responding to different scenarios in a controlled environment. This helps build decision-making skills as well as impulse control. Role-playing can also be a simple way for students to figure out appropriate behavior. One 1st grade teacher I know kept a bag full of hypothetical scenarios to role-play (e.g., "You can't get your jacket unzipped," "Someone took your pencil off your desk," "Your classmate just called you a mean name") that students could draw from. For older students, use scenarios that require more complex problem solving.

Be specific about what you want your students to glean from this experience. An ideal time to use role-play is at the beginning or end of a unit of study. Students enjoy dressing up as historical or literary figures, and role-playing is a good way to foster understanding of different perspectives. When role-playing scenarios with others, students can also switch roles to see the same situation from different points of view.

Believe it or not, research has found that students who role-play as superheroes perform better at school (White et al., 2017). The researchers refer to this as the "Batman effect" and claim that students who pretend to be a superhero show improved cognitive flexibility. The study notes that children use the same brain networks when they play pretend and transfer skills they develop that way for use in real-life contexts. It stands to reason that *imagining* we're strong, powerful, and confident can help us *feel* strong, powerful, and confident!

Brain Breaks

According to Judy Willis (2016b), for every 20 to 30 minutes of focused attention, it is necessary for teenagers to have a 3- to 5-minute break. When our brains become fatigued, we get stressed and our attention fades. Short breaks revitalize our neural connections, helping students to feel refreshed and energized to continue learning. Here are some strategies to consider:

- **The balloon challenge.** Students stand in a circle around you as you blow up a balloon. Toss the balloon in the air and challenge students to keep it off the ground by using their feet, heads, elbows, knees, or any other body part except their hands.
- **Thinking outside the box.** Start a drawing on the whiteboard and ask students to take turns completing it, telling them it cannot be a box. Challenge them by either starting an unusual object or having a student begin the drawing with anything from a few lines to a squiggle.
- **Reflection.** Turn on some soft music, dim the lights, and have students close their eyes and take steady breaths. You may give them a prompt on which to reflect (e.g., "Think about something positive

that happened today") or allow them to reflect on something of their choice.
- **Puzzles.** Buy some small, inexpensive puzzles and have students work in pairs to put them together. Though this only takes a couple of minutes, it relaxes the parts of the brain that they have been using. If they have been focused on a specific topic or project, the prefrontal cortex will be given time to reset, and the networks of neurons that might be depleted of some neurotransmitters can be replenished.
- **Would you rather?** For this activity, students work in small groups and discuss some questions that you make up—for example, "Would you rather have your favorite singer or your favorite fictional character move in next door?" or "If you could choose only one, would you rather have lunch or dinner?" To make this brain break more active, read the question aloud to the class and ask students to go to designated corners representing their answers.
- **Explanations.** This is a fun, rapid-fire activity. To the whole class, make a statement like "My car has a dent in the passenger door." Then ask either "What happened to it?" or "What's your excuse?" Randomly choose students to answer the question. You might get responses like "You parked too close to the car next to you" and "A bird flew into the door." As students get more creative with answers, you will hear lots of laughter and some crazy explanations.

Problem Solving

Effective problem solving involves planning, goal setting, prioritization, time management, and organization. Setbacks teach students to regulate their emotions in the face of difficulties, contributing to their emotional resilience. Problem solving inherently involves making decisions, so students learn to weigh options, consider consequences, and make informed choices.

Consider explicitly teaching problem solving by presenting a problem, brainstorming solutions, picking one, testing it, and reviewing the results. Have the students make a chart listing the problem-solving steps to hang in the room and refer to it often.

Another option for younger students is to introduce problem-solving games that require children to consider multiple solutions, like riddles, guessing games, and card games such as UNO. Encourage students to discuss different approaches and celebrate creative problem solving. Here are a few examples of hypothetical problems you might work through:

- It's your birthday, and you usually invite your classmates to your house for cake after school. However, a new student has joined your class, and you are not acquainted with them. Do you invite them to your party?
- Your alarm didn't go off, and you woke up 30 minutes late. You must submit your assignment before school starts, or you will be penalized. What should you do?
- While taking an important test, your pencil breaks. You can't talk during the test, or you will get in trouble. What should you do?

Establish Routines and Expectations

Clear routines and expectations establish the sense of predictability that all students need. Knowing what to expect and what is expected of them sets the stage for improvements in executive functioning by lowering stress levels.

One effective routine to implement is communicating transitions between activities—sometimes the brain needs concrete information to switch focus. Get everyone's attention before asking them to switch to a new activity or place in the room. Class rules and norms should be posted in sight for your students, including rules for curbing impulsive actions (e.g., "Always raise your hand to ask for help"). You may even consider leading your students in compiling these lists. Be sure to define each rule: For example, what does it mean to "Use materials appropriately"? Consider the tools in your classroom; scissors, for example, need training in appropriate use. Ask your students (older as well as younger!) how to hold them and hand them to others, and make sure they know never to run with scissors. Students could make posters listing the rules and norms they help develop, younger students using drawings rather than words.

Visual Aids

Visual aids in the form of charts, diagrams, or interactive displays allow students to double-check the information in their working memories and make for a more holistic and inclusive learning experience:

- Younger students can use visual prompts to identify and express their emotions, supporting the development of self-awareness and self-management skills.
- Visual representations of goals and progress charts provide a tangible way for students to track their achievements, support goal setting and self-monitoring, and help foster a sense of accomplishment and motivation.
- Visual schedules and routine charts serve as consistent reminders of daily tasks and expectations, help students develop time-management skills, and contribute to the establishment of a structured learning environment.
- A visual agenda can help students understand the amount of time they'll need to spend on a topic, see what is going to happen next, and help them to plan their time and energy accordingly.
- Use visual timers to help younger students understand the concept of time. These can also help with practice delaying immediate gratification.
- Flowcharts and problem-solving diagrams can guide students through the steps of critical thinking and decision making.

Mindfulness

Mindfulness involves paying attention to our thoughts, emotions, and sensations in the present moment without judgment. Practicing mindfulness

- Cultivates self-awareness by making us more attuned to our thoughts and emotions (a fundamental element of developing executive functions);
- Fosters self-regulation;
- Enhances attention and concentration;
- Reduces stress levels;

- Helps develop resilience and perseverance; and
- Promotes a sense of community, trust, and collaboration.

Dunning and colleagues (2019) note that mindfulness increases the number of neurons in the prefrontal lobe while decreasing the number in the amygdala, which supports cognitive flexibility. Here are a few mindfulness practices to implement in the classroom, preferably at the very beginning or end of class:

- **Mindful breathing.** Have students follow these steps:
  1. Take a slow breath in through the nose, breathing into your lower belly for about four seconds.
  2. Hold your breath for one or two seconds.
  3. Exhale slowly through the mouth for about four or five seconds.
  4. Wait a few seconds and repeat.
- **Mindful listening.** Students close their eyes and focus on various sounds around them. Afterward, they discuss their experiences and how it felt to be fully present in the moment.
- **Mindful walking.** Take students outside and encourage them to walk slowly, paying attention to each step and the sensations in their feet. This simple activity connects movement with mindfulness.
- **Mindful gratitude.** Students stand or sit in a circle and each shares one thing they are grateful for.

Time Management

Introduce students to time-management tools such as planners or organizational apps and teach them how to break down larger assignments into manageable chunks. Consider sharing a scenario like this one to drive home the importance of time management:

> You have 60 minutes to do the following: answer 20 math problems, finish your laundry, and take out the garbage. How will you get this all done? What will you do first, second, and last? Which of these is the most important to you? How much time will you allocate for each?

This can be a great group discussion in which students with time-management difficulties may hear helpful suggestions from their peers. Tell them they have 10 minutes to discuss and set a timer so they stick to it.

Teach Your Students About Their Brains

The more your students understand how their brains work, the easier it will be for them to understand executive functions. You may wish to show older students the wonderful *The Adventures of You* series of videos that introduces students to executive functions and the prefrontal cortex and their effect on life and career decision making. The series was made by myfuture Australia (2021); videos and support materials are available at https://myfuture.edu.au/career-articles/details/making-good-career-decisions-the-adventures-of-you.

Appendix B: Modeling

Following are some recommended ways to model the various SEL skills and EFS discussed in this book.

Think-Alouds

Narrate your thought process when faced with decisions that require you to leverage your executive function skills. For example:

> I can't believe I forgot to reserve the small gym for our play practice! I want to march down there and tell Mr. Martin that he can't use it for his class because our practice is much more important. I want to scream at the top of my lungs! But none of that is going to do any good. I need to find another time for us to have the cafeteria. I'm taking some deep breaths, just like I've asked you all to do so many times. We will break into small groups here in the classroom, rehearse our lines, and I'll see if I can arrange for a large room of some kind for tomorrow. I'm sorry I messed up.

Real-Life Examples

Share real-life examples, including personal stories, in which EFS are successfully leveraged. Discuss the positive outcomes that resulted from thoughtful decision making. For example:

> I was driving to school this morning, and I ended up behind a school bus. That made me a little crazy as I was in a hurry to get here and knew I would have to stop several times as the bus picked up students. So, I was stressed and got more stressed each time the

bus stopped. I couldn't go around it, and there were no side streets on that long strip around the park. At the last pickup, a parent came out to the bus with their student and started a conversation with the bus driver. I couldn't believe this was happening! I really wanted to honk the horn, but something told me that this conversation was important. I moved my hand away from the horn, and I'm glad I did. And you know what? I got to school in plenty of time!

Pausing Before Responding

This is especially helpful for impulse inhibition, working memory, and cognitive flexibility. Emphasize the importance of pausing before responding to a stimulus. Model the behavior of stopping, thinking, and reflecting before making a decision or reacting impulsively. Consider the power of wait time as well: It is recommended that you wait three to five seconds after asking a question for a student to respond, then again before continuing once the student is done. Share this formula with students and discuss how waiting before responding can inhibit impulsivity.

Decision Making and Problem Solving

Discuss the importance of weighing pros and cons, considering consequences, and making intentional choices. Model how to think through decisions systematically.

Consider the following scenario. Out of nowhere in class, 8th grade teacher Mrs. Murphy finds herself distraught about the remodeling of her kitchen.

"I'm having a little trouble focusing today," she says at the beginning of class. "My kitchen is completely torn apart and I can't even cook! If I don't decide on which countertop to order, we're never going to finish this project. If I choose quartz, I'll never be able to put a hot pan on the countertop again because it will scorch it. If I choose the granite, it's going to cost more than my budget will allow."

"Make a list of the pros and cons," a student offers. Mrs. Murphy asks that student to go to the whiteboard, and as a class they discuss the pros and cons of different countertops. By the end of the class, the students feel they have contributed to her decision themselves and can go through a similar process when they have their own decisions to make.

Appropriate Emotional Expression

Model how to express emotions in a healthy and controlled manner. Show that it's OK to feel emotions, but also demonstrate how to manage and express them in a way that considers others. For example, after your class has been interrupted by a messenger from the office or a fire drill, you might mention to your students that you were unhappy with the disruption, but you know these things happen and you try to pick up where you left off. You could ask students, "How do you feel at the end of the day when you've just received your fourth homework assignment? Do you feel like yelling at your teacher? Would that be helpful? When I get angry or frustrated, I might imagine myself losing control and throwing something or yelling at someone, and if I just imagine that without actually doing it, there's no harm done. Then I might call a friend to talk to about it. Would anyone like to share how they react when they feel frustrated?" Watching your reactions and listening to others' stories provides ideas for healthy expression.

Long-Term Goals

Talk about long-term goals and the EFS necessary for achieving them. Model delaying immediate gratification and share about the Stanford marshmallow test with students. Ask questions such as "What would the treat need to be to make you wait for a second one?" "What would you be unable to resist?" or "What strategies could you use to help you wait for another treat?" Share goals of your own related to teaching or classroom management, and periodically discuss your progress with students.

Feedback

Model how to seek and receive feedback by asking your students for their opinions on a particular teaching method or activity. Demonstrate how to process the feedback constructively, and consider adjustments for improvement. It might go something like this: "What did you think of the jigsaw activity we just did? Raise your hand if you liked it, and I can call on you to tell us why." After listening to one or two positive accounts, say, "Thank you for that feedback. Now, raise your hand if you didn't like it and would like to explain why." After a couple of negative accounts, if students want to discuss those responses, let them do so. Then say something like, "I appreciate your comments. I like jigsaws because everyone gets a chance to participate. I will consider all your feedback when I am thinking of doing this activity again."

Personal Boundaries

Model how to assertively communicate your needs and preferences rather than react impulsively to situations that may compromise those boundaries. Have students talk to one another about their boundaries. When students appear to need some personal space from you or the class, respect that need, and let students know that you are doing so: "Josh needs some time to himself and will join his group when he feels comfortable doing so."

Growth Mindset

Emphasize the idea that skills can be developed over time. Model a growth mindset by showing that improvement is possible with effort and practice. Sharing your own mistakes with students will strengthen your relationships with them and bring you all closer as they see you have something in common with them. For example:

> Ms. Johnson puts different geography trivia on the board each day for her 7th graders. The first time she made a spelling error, the students teased her and laughed. She looked at them and said, "Your teasing is irritating, and I feel annoyed at you. But I know I didn't look over my work as I should have. Let's remember that our brains learn from mistakes. I will remember now to read over the statements or questions I put on the board." Ms. Johnson told me that she purposely makes mistakes now, and the class laughs about them as students compete to find her errors.

Memory Strategies

Demonstrate using acronyms, rhymes, or other mnemonic devices to remember information. For example, you can explain how the acronym HOMES helps you remember the names of the Great Lakes (Huron,

Ontario, Michigan, Erie, and Superior). You might also teach students about the "method of loci" visualization technique that involves picturing what you want to remember in a specific place. For example, you might say the following:

> As you walk into the room, the first thing you see is the window. Picture a person climbing out of that window to help you remember the protagonist of the book you're reading. Then, as your gaze leaves the window, you see my desk. You might picture a miniature town on the desk to help you remember the story's setting. Next, you notice the bookshelf. Picture two students fighting over a book to represent conflict. On the bulletin board, you might picture numbers 1, 2, and 3 to represent events in the plot. Finally, we need to remember theme, or the central idea of the story. Just past the bulletin board is the reading corner. The lamp by the chair can represent theme, as ideas are often represented by lightbulbs.

Breaking Tasks into Manageable Steps

Model the technique of chunking information by breaking it into smaller, manageable parts or steps. This is particularly useful for remembering longer sequences or lists. For example, you can demonstrate how you remember telephone numbers with 10 numerals (going beyond the 7 bits of information that working memory has been thought to hold) by chunking the 10 numerals into 3 bits: the area code, the first three digits of the phone number, and then the last four digits. You would think of the phone number 555-123-4567 as the three parts 555, 123, and 4567. In the classroom, this strategy can be as simple as making assignments shorter, like asking students to read the first 10 pages of the chapter for tomorrow rather than the whole chapter, or giving two 5-word spelling tests instead of one 10-word test.

Multisensory Techniques

Try to engage multiple senses when presenting information by incorporating visuals, auditory cues, and hands-on activities to reinforce learning and activate different parts of the brain. For example, using felt letters as you teach letter sounds to younger students engages touch, hearing, and vision. As the students trace the letters and hear the sounds, they are activating the phonological loop, the visual-spatial sketchpad, and the attentional system (Dehaene, 2009).

Diverse Perspectives

Introduce diverse perspectives in your teaching materials and discuss how different cultures, backgrounds, and experiences contribute to varied ways of thinking. Facilitate group discussions where students can share and compare their perspectives. Model active listening and demonstrate open-mindedness by being receptive to diverse ideas and opinions.

Checklists

When planning activities or organizing classroom materials, make it a point to use checklists visibly. Explain the purpose of each checklist and how it helps you keep track of tasks. Emphasize the satisfaction of checking items off the list upon completion.

References

Aeon, B., Faber, A., & Panaccio, A. (2021). Does time management work? A meta-analysis. *PLOS One, 16*(1). https://journals.plos.org/plosone/article?id=10.1371/journal.pone.0245066

Amen, D., Amen, C., & Castellanos, A. (2019). *Change your brain, change your grades: The secrets of successful students: Science-based strategies to boost memory, strengthen focus, and study faster*. BenBella Books.

Aspen Institute National Commission on Social, Emotional, and Academic Development. (2019). *From a nation at risk to a nation of hope*. Author. https://files.eric.ed.gov/fulltext/ED606337.pdf

Attia, P. (2023). *Outlive: The science and art of longevity*. Harmony.

Barkley, R. (2020). *12 principles for raising a child with ADHD*. Guilford.

Beachboard, C. (2019, December 11). Promoting prosocial behaviors in the classroom. *Edutopia*. https://www.edutopia.org/article/promoting-prosocial-behaviors-classroom/

Best, J. R., & Miller, P. H. (2010). A developmental perspective on executive function. *Child Development, 81*(6), 1641–1660.

Bezdjian, S., Baker, L., & Tuvblad, C. (2011). Genetic and environmental influences on impulsivity: A meta-analysis of twin, family and adoption studies. *Clinical Psychology Review, 31*(7), 1209–1223.

Blair, C., & Raver, C. C. (2016). Poverty, stress, and brain development: New directions for prevention and intervention. *Academic Pediatrics, 16*(3 Suppl.), S30–S36.

Bornstein, D. (2018, January 30). Treating the lifelong harm of childhood trauma. *The New York Times*. https://www.nytimes.com/2018/01/30/opinion/treating-the-lifelong-harm-of-childhood-trauma.html

Brackett, M. (2019). *Permission to feel: The power of emotional intelligence to achieve well-being and success*. New York: Celadon.

Brafman, O. (2011, April 20). How to build instant connections [Video lecture]. *Entrepreneurial Thought Leaders: A Stanford Speaker Series*. https://ecorner.stanford.edu/videos/how-to-build-instant-connections-entire-talk/

Brown, P. C., Roediger, H. L., III, & McDaniel, M. A. (2014). *Make it stick: The science of successful learning*. Belknap.

Burke Harris, N. (2018). *The deepest well: Healing the long-term effects of childhood adversity*. Mariner.

Busch, B. (Ed.). (n.d.). 5 ways educators can support neurodiverse students. *InnerDrive*. https://www.innerdrive.co.uk/blog/support-neurodiverse-students/

Calarco, J. (2018, June 1). Why rich kids are so good at the marshmallow test. *The Atlantic*. https://www.theatlantic.com/family/archive/2018/06/marshmallow-test/561779/

Carlson, S., White, R., & Davis-Unger, A. (2014, January–March). Evidence for a relation between executive function and pretense representation in preschool children. *Cognitive Development, 29*, 1–16.

CASEL. (n.d.). *Fundamentals of SEL*. https://casel.org/fundamentals-of-sel/

Center on the Developing Child at Harvard University. (n.d.). *Executive function and self-regulation*. https://developingchild.harvard.edu/science/key-concepts/executive-function/#:~:text=Executive%20function%20and%20self%2Dregulation,and%20juggle%20multiple%20tasks%20successfully

Center on the Developing Child at Harvard University. (2011). *Building the brain's "air traffic control" system: How early experiences shape the development of executive function: Working paper no. 11*. https://developingchild.harvard.edu/wp-content/uploads/2011/05/How-Early-Experiences-Shape-the-Development-of-Executive-Function.pdf

Center on the Developing Child at Harvard University. (2012). *InBrief: Executive function*. https://developingchild.harvard.edu/resources/inbrief-executive-function

Center on the Developing Child at Harvard University. (2014). *Activities guide: Enhancing and practicing executive function skills with children from infancy to adolescence*. https://developingchild.harvard.edu/resources/activities-guide-enhancing-and-practicing-executive-function-skills-with-children-from-infancy-to-adolescence/

Cipriano, C., Strambler, M. J., Naples, L. H., Ha, C., Kirk, M., Wood, M., Sehgal, K., Zieher, A. K., Eveleigh, A., McCarthy, M., Funaro, M., Ponnock, A., Chow, J. C., & Durlak, J. (2023). The state of evidence for social and emotional learning: A contemporary meta-analysis of universal school-based SEL interventions. *Child Development, 94*(5), 1181–1204.

Cleveland Clinic. (n.d.). *Executive dysfunction*. https://my.clevelandclinic.org/health/symptoms/23224-executive-dysfunction

Csikszentmihalyi, M. (2008). *Flow: The psychology of optimal experience*. Harper Perennial Modern Classics.

Dabbagh, N., & Kitsantas, A. (2012). Personal learning environments, social media, and self-regulated learning: A natural formula for connecting formal and informal learning. *The Internet and Higher Education, 15*(1), 3–8.

Darling-Hammond, L., Flook, L., Cook-Harvey, C., Barron, B., & Osher, D. (2020). Implications for educational practice of the science of learning and development. *Applied Developmental Science, 24*(2), 97–140.

Dehaene, S. (2009). *Reading in the brain: The science and evolution of a human invention*. New York: Viking Adult.

Desautels, L. L. (2024). *Intentional neuroplasticity: Moving our nervous systems and educational system toward post-traumatic growth*. Wyatt-MacKenzie.

deWilde, A., Koot, H., & Van Lier, P. (2016). Developmental links between children's working memory and their social relations with teachers and peers in the early school years. *Journal of Abnormal Child Psychology, 44*(1), 19–30.

Diamond, A. (2014). Want to optimize executive functions and academic outcomes? Simple, just nourish the human spirit. *Minnesota Symposium on Child Psychology, 37,* 205–232.

Diamond, A. (2021, December 14). *Optimizing executive functions in children and adults with ADHD* [Webinar]. ADDitude. https://www.additudemag.com/webinar/executive-functions-adhd-children-adults-podcast-383

Diamond, A., & Lee, K. (2011). Interventions shown to aid executive function development in children 4 to 12 years old. *Science, 333*(6045), 959–964.

Duckworth, A. L., Peterson, C., Matthews, M. D., & Kelly, D. R. (2007). Grit: Perseverance and passion for long-term goals. *Journal of Personality and Social Psychology, 92*(6), 1087–1101.

Dunning, D. L., Griffiths, K., Kuyken, W., Crane, C., Foulkes, L., Parker, J., & Dalgleish, T. (2019, March). Research review: The effects of mindfulness-based interventions on cognition and mental health in children and adolescents—A meta-analysis of randomized controlled trials. *Journal of Child Psychology and Psychiatry, 60*(3), 244–258.

Evans, S. W., Allan, D., Xiang, J., Margherio, S. M., Owens, J. S., & Langberg, J. M. (2021, August). Organization interventions as a mediator of change in grades in the Challenging Horizons Program. *Journal of School Psychology, 87,* 18–27.

Fisher, A. V., Godwin, K. E., & Seltman, H. (2014). Visual environment, attention allocation, and learning: When too much of a good thing may be bad. *Psychological Science, 25*(7), 1362–1370.

Friedman, N. P., & Miyake, A. (2017). Unity and diversity of executive functions: Individual differences as a window on cognitive structure. *Cortex, 86,* 186–204.

Friedman, N. P., & Robbins, T. W. (2022). The role of prefrontal cortex in cognitive control and executive function. *Neuropsychopharmacology, 47,* 72–89.

Gendron, M. (n.d.). *An in-depth look at executive functioning: Self-monitoring* [Online learning module]. LD@school. https://www.ldatschool.ca/learning-modules/executive-functions/eight-pillars/self-monitoring

Goleman, D. (1994). *Emotional intelligence: Why it can matter more than IQ.* Bantam.

Guare, R., Dawson, P., & Guare, C. (2013). *Smart but scattered teens: The "executive skills" program for helping teens reach their potential.* Guilford.

Guo, L. (2022). The effects of self-monitoring on strategy use and academic performance: A meta-analysis. *International Journal of Educational Research, 112.*

Hanover Research. (2016). *Early skills and predictors of academic success.* Author. https://portal.ct.gov/-/media/SDE/ESSA-Evidence-Guides/Early_Skills_and_Predictors_of_Academic_Success

Harvard Health Publishing. (2021, February 15). Protect your brain from stress. https://www.health.harvard.edu/mind-and-mood/protect-your-brain-from-stress

Jacobson, R. (2023, October 30). What is working memory? Understanding our mental "scratchpad." Child Mind Institute. https://childmind.org/article/what-is-working-memory

Jagers, R. J., Skoog-Hoffman, A., Barthelus, B., & Schlund, J. (2021, Summer). Transformative social and emotional learning. *American Educator.* https://www.aft.org/ae/summer2021/jagers_skoog-hoffman_barthelus_schlund

Johnson, L. E., & Lambert, M. C. (2011). Learned helplessness. In S. Goldstein & J. A. Naglieri (Eds.), *Encyclopedia of child behavior and development* (pp. 871–872). Springer.

Kemna, A. (2022, October 7). How to deal with executive dysfunction at work. *Best Colleges*. https://www.bestcolleges.com/careers/dealing-with-executive-dysfunction-at-work/

Larmer, J. (2015, July 13). Project-based learning vs. problem-based learning vs. X-BL. *Edutopia*. https://www.edutopia.org/blog/pbl-vs-pbl-vs-xbl-john-larmer

Liu, H., & Li, H. (2020, March 26). Self-control modulates the behavioral response of interpersonal forgiveness. *Frontiers in Psychology, 11*.

Low, R. (2021, February 10). Improving social-emotional learning by teaching executive function. *EdWeb.net*. https://home.edweb.net/improving-social-emotional-learning-by-teaching-executive-function

Lukasik, K. M., Waris, O., Soveri, A., Lehtonen, M., & Laine, M. (2019, January 23). The relationship of anxiety and stress with working memory performance in a large non-depressed sample. *Frontiers in Psychology, 10*(4).

Macmillan, C. (2020, November 6). Why social and emotional learning is so important for kids right now. *Yale Medicine*. https://www.yalemedicine.org/news/social-emotional-child-development

Marks, G. (2023). *Attention span*. Hanover Square.

Mathy, F., Chekaf, M., & Cowan, N. (2018, May 25). Simple and complex working memory tasks allow similar benefits of information compression. *Journal of Cognition, 1*(1), 31.

McCarver-Reyes, M. (2019, February 21). Revelations about sleep and impulsivity in young adults. *MedPage Today*. https://www.medpagetoday.com/resource-centers/excessive-sleepiness-and-associated-risks-with-obstructive-sleep-apnea/revelations-sleep-and-impulsivity-young-adults/2425

Medina, J. (2018). *Attack of the teenage brain! Understanding and supporting the weird and wonderful adolescent learner*. ASCD.

Medina, J. (2020). *Brain rules: 12 principles for surviving and thriving at work, home, and school*. Pear Press.

Minahan, J. (2019). Trauma-informed teaching strategies. *Educational Leadership, 77*(2). https://www.ascd.org/el/articles/trauma-informed-teaching-strategies

Mitchell, M. R., & Potenza, M. N. (2014, September 20). Recent insights into the neurobiology of impulsivity. *Current Addiction Reports, 1*, 309–319. https://link.springer.com/article/10.1007/s40429-014-0037-4

Moore, A., & Malinowski, P. (2009, March). Meditation, mindfulness and cognitive flexibility. *Consciousness and Cognition, 18*(1), 176–186.

Murphy, M. (2018, April 15). Neuroscience explains why you need to write down your goals if you actually want to achieve them. *Forbes*. https://www.forbes.com/sites/markmurphy/2018/04/15/neuroscience-explains-why-you-need-to-write-down-your-goals-if-you-actually-want-to-achieve-them/

myfuture Australia. (2021, August 5). Making good career decisions: The adventures of you. https://myfuture.edu.au/career-articles/details/making-good-career-decisions-the-adventures-of-you

National Institute of Mental Health. (2023). *The teen brain: 7 things to know*. U.S. Department of Health and Human Services. https://www.nimh.nih.gov/health/publications/the-teen-brain-7-things-to-know

OWN. (2011, October 19). *The powerful lesson Maya Angelou taught Oprah* [Video]. https://www.oprah.com/oprahs-lifeclass/the-powerful-lesson-maya-angelou-taught-oprah-video

Perry, B. D. (2023, August 29). Building a connected classroom [Video]. *ThinkTVPBS.* https://www.youtube.com/watch?v=yhxxZWJNhhQ

Perry, B. D., & Szalavitz, M. (2007). *The boy who was raised as a dog and other stories from a child psychiatrist's notebook: What traumatized children can teach us about loss, love, and healing.* Basic Books.

Perry, B. D., & Winfrey, O. (2021). *What happened to you? Conversations on trauma, resilience, and healing.* Flatiron Books.

Pochon, J. B., Levy, R., Poline, J. B., Crozier, S., Lehéricy, S., Pillon, B., Deweer, B., Le Bihan, D., & Dubois, B. (2001). The role of dorsolateral prefrontal cortex in the preparation of forthcoming actions: An fMRI study. *Cerebral Cortex, 11*(3), 260–266.

Porter, L. (2002). Cognitive skills. In L. Porter (Ed.), *Educating young children with special needs* (pp. 191–209). Sage.

Rimm-Kaufman, S., & Sandilos, L. (2015). *Improving students' relationships with teachers to provide essential supports for learning: Applications of psychological science to teaching and learning modules.* American Psychological Association. https://www.apa.org/education-career/k12/relationships

Sampalo, M., Lázaro, E., & Luna, P. M. (2023, March). Action video gaming and attention in young adults: A systematic review. *Journal of Attention Disorders, 27*(5), 530–538.

Schmitt, S. A., Korucu, I., Purpura, D. J., Whiteman, S., Zhang, C., & Yang, F. (2019). Exploring cross-cultural variations in the development of executive function for preschoolers from low and high socioeconomic families. *International Journal of Behavioral Development, 43*(3), 212–220.

Scieszka, J. (2014). *The true story of the three little pigs* (L. Smith, Illus.; 25th anniversary ed.). Viking.

Scionti, N., Cavallero, M., Zogmaister, C., & Marzocchi, G. M. (2020, January 9). Is cognitive training effective for improving executive functions in preschoolers? A systematic review and meta-analysis. *Frontiers in Psychology, 10.*

Searle, M. (2013). *Causes and cures in the classroom: Getting to the root of academic and behavior problems.* ASCD.

Shafer, L. (2016, July 15). What makes SEL work? *Usable Knowledge.* Harvard Graduate School of Education. https://www.gse.harvard.edu/ideas/usable-knowledge/16/07/what-makes-sel-work

Sinclair, K. (2023, January 19). Executive function skills: Which EF skills should I see at different ages? *EF Specialists.* https://www.efspecialists.com/post/executive-function-skills-which-ef-skills-should-i-see-at-different-ages

Sippl, A. (2020). Executive functioning skills 101: The basics of planning. *Life Skills Advocate.* https://lifeskillsadvocate.com/blog/executive-functioning-skills-101-the-basics-of-planning/

Sleek, S. (2015, August 31). *How poverty affects the brain and behavior.* Association for Psychological Science. https://www.psychologicalscience.org/observer/how-poverty-affects-the-brain-and-behavior

Smith, S. W. (2002). *Applying cognitive-behavioral techniques to social skills instruction* (ED469279). ERIC/OSEP Digest. ERIC Clearinghouse on Disabilities and Gifted Education. https://files.eric.ed.gov/fulltext/ED469279.pdf

Southwest Institute for Emotional Intelligence. (2018, June 21). *Lack of impulse control: Is it preventing leaders from engaging with their team?* Author. https://www.swiei.com/2018/06/21

Sparks, S. D. (2019, March 12). Why teacher-student relationships matter. *Education Week.* https://www.edweek.org/teaching-learning/why-teacher-student-relationships-matter/2019/03

Sprenger, M. (2020). *Social-emotional learning and the brain: Strategies to help your students thrive.* ASCD.

Takeuchi, H., Taki, Y., Sassa, Y., Hashizume, H., Sekiguchi, A., Fukushima, A., & Kawashima, R. (2011, August 23). Working memory training using mental calculation impacts regional gray matter of the frontal and parietal regions. *PLoS One, 6*(8).

Taren, A. A., Gianaros, P. J., Greco, C. M., Lindsay, E. K., Fairgrieve, A., Brown, K. W., Rosen, R. K., Ferris, J. L., Julson, E., Marsland, A. L., Bursley, J. K., Ramsburg, J., & Creswell, J. D. (2015). Mindfulness meditation training alters stress-related amygdala resting state functional connectivity: A randomized controlled trial. *Social Cognitive and Affective Neuroscience, 10*(12), 1758–1768.

Trentepohl, S., Waldeyer, J., Fleischer, J., Roelle, J., Leutner, D., & Wirth, J. (2022). How did it get so late so soon? The effects of time management knowledge and practice on students' time management skills and academic performance. *Sustainability, 14*(9), 5097.

Tull, M. (2023). Impulse control disorder and impulsive behavior. *Very Well Mind.* https://www.verywellmind.com/impulse-control-disorder-impulsive-behavior-2797366

van der Kolk, B. (2015). *The body keeps the score: Brain, mind, and body in the healing of trauma.* Penguin.

Vitiello, V. E., Nguyen, T., Ruzek, E., Pianta, R. C., & Whittaker, J. V. (2022). Differences between preK and kindergarten classroom experiences: Do they predict children's social-emotional skills and self-regulation across the transition to kindergarten? *Early Childhood Research Quarterly, 59,* 287–299. https://www.sciencedirect.com/science/article/abs/pii/S0885200621001393?dgcid=auth

Vogel, S., & Schwabe, L. (2016). Learning and memory under stress: Implications for the classroom. *npj Science of Learning.* https://www.nature.com/articles/npjscilearn201611

Ward, C. M. (2020). What are normal attention spans for children? *The Kid's Directory Family Resource Guide.* https://www.kids-houston.com/normal-attention-spans-for-kids/

White, R. E., & Carlson, S. M. (2021, July). Pretending with realistic and fantastical stories facilitates executive function in 3-year-old children. *Journal of Experimental Child Psychology, 207.*

White, R. E., Prager, E. O., Schaefer, C., Kross, E., Duckworth, A. L., & Carlson, S. M. (2017, September). The "Batman effect": Improving perseverance in young children. *Child Development, 88*(5), 1563–1571.

Willis, J. (2016a). Building students' cognitive flexibility. *Edutopia.* https://www.edutopia.org/blog/building-students-cognitive-flexibility-judy-willis

Willis, J. (2016b). Using brain breaks to restore students' focus. *Edutopia*. https://www.edutopia.org/article/brain-breaks-restore-student-focus-judy-willis

Willis, J., & Willis, M. (2020). *Research-based strategies to ignite student learning: Insights from neuroscience and the classroom (Revised and expanded ed.)*. ASCD.

Yucel, Ö., Karahoca, D., & Karahoca, A. (2016). The effects of problem-based learning on cognitive flexibility, self-regulation skills and students' achievements. *Global Journal of Information Technology, 6*(1), 86–93.

Zelazo, P. D., & Carlson, S. M. (2020). The neurodevelopment of executive function skills: Implications for academic achievement gaps. *Psychology & Neuroscience, 13*(3), 273–298.

Index

Note: Page references followed by an italicized *f* indicate information contained in figures.

academic domain, 8
academic goals lists, 85
accountability partner system, 77
The Adventures of You (video series), 103
adverse childhood experiences, 10
agency, 89, 94
agenda, daily, displayed, 26
alarms, 86
alarm system, 9
amygdala, 10, 35
anterior cingulate gyrus, 57
arousal system, 9
assessment and monitoring, 92
assignment length, 40–41
attention and focus, 4, 13, 44–46
    average attention span by age, 46*f*
    research findings, 47–48
    SEL connection, 48–50, 49*f*, 91
    self-assessment, 51*f*
    strategies for older students, 53–54
    strategies for younger students, 51–53
    timeline of development, 47
authority, pushback against, 24

balloon challenge activity, 98
basal ganglia, 35
Batman effect, 98
behavioral interventions, 92
belonging, 90
brain breaks, 41, 98–99
brain functions, teaching about, 103
brainstorming sessions, 64
breathing, 22
broken relationships, 24
buddy system, 27, 74, 75*f*

calendars, 86
celebrations and appreciations, 27, 77
cerebellum, 35
checklists, 109
chunking information, 41
chunking projects, 85
classroom contracts, 29
classroom designated areas, 26
classroom jobs, 74
classroom rules and norms, 100
class rules posters, 25
cognitive flexibility, 4, 13, 56
    characteristics of underdeveloped, 58–60
    defined, 57
    research findings, 56–58
    SEL connection, 59*f*, 91
    self-assessment, 61*f*

cognitive flexibility (*cont'd*)
   strategies for older students,
     63–66
   strategies for younger students,
     60–63
   timeline of development, 57–58
cognitive regulation skills, 8
Collaborative for Academic, Social,
   and Emotional Learning (CASEL), 2
collaborative problem solving, 90
communication, 11, 27
communication styles, 60
community involvement, 93
community service projects, 29
complex task avoidance, 39
conflict negotiation, 11
cooperation, 11
creative writing prompts, 64
critical thinking, 29, 64
cue cards, 74
curiosity, 90
curriculum alignment, 92

deadlines, 26, 85
debates, 63
debriefing strategies, 77
decision making, responsible.
   See responsible decision making
detail, inattention to, 72
digital span tasks, 39–40
disorganization, 83
distractions, limiting, 39
diverse perspectives, 109
Dual N-Back game, 42–43

emotional domain, 8
emotional expression, appropriate,
   106
emotional expression, student, 26
emotional intelligence, 8
emotional memory, 35
emotional state, 9
emotion cards, 74
emotion recognition, 62
emotion word list, 22*f*
empathy, 11, 24
encoding, 33
environment and culture, 93

episodic memory, 35
ethical dilemma discussions, 65
executive function games, 63
executive function skills. *See also*
   specific skills
   brain breaks, 98–99
   establish routines and
     expectations, 100
   executive dysfunction, 14
   mindfulness, 101–102
   neurological basis of, 15–16
   problem solving, 99–100
   promoting to parents and
     communities, 93–94
   role-play, 97–98
   and SEL, 90–91
   self-assessment for staff and
     teachers, 95–96, 95*f*
   skills, 2–4, 13–15
   strategies to foster, 97–103
   time management, 102
   and transformative SEL, 94–95
   visual aids, 101
executive state, 9
exit tickets, 42
expectations, 100
experiential learning, 65
explanations activity, 99
explicit instruction, 92
explicit (declarative) memory, 35

feedback, 27, 60, 72, 76, 106–107
fidgety behaviors, 24
fight, flight, or freeze response, 9
flexible seating, 74
focus. *See* attention and focus
following instructions, 71
forgetfulness, 38, 83

games and activities, 27
goal setting, 10, 72, 76, 86
goal-setting activities, 65
gratitude journals, 12
grouping, flexible, 64
group storytelling, 27
growth mindset, 107
guest speakers, 29, 65

hypothetical situations, 64

identity, 89
impatience, 23
implicit (nondeclarative) memory, 35
improvisational games, 61
impulse control, 10
impulse inhibition, 3, 13, 17–18, 29–30
   characteristics of
      underdeveloped, 23–24
   emotion word list, 22*f*
   research findings, 18–20
   SEL connection, 20–23, 21*f*, 90
   self-assessment, 24, 25*f*
   and self-monitoring, 71
   and self-regulation, 90
   Stanford marshmallow test, 19–20
   strategies for older students,
      28–29
   strategies for preventing
      impulsive behaviors, 23
   strategies for younger students,
      25–28
   timeline of development for, 19
inappropriate talk, 24
inattentiveness, 38
inclusive practices, 92
inconsistent performance, 71
individualized scaffolding, 76
information presentation, 41, 60
instructional length, 74
instructions, following, 23, 38
interdisciplinary learning, 63–64
interpersonal skills, 8
interruptions, 23

journaling, 28, 65, 76

kindness, 12
knowledge transfer, 60
KWL charts, 41

lack of understanding, 23
listening, 11
long-term goals, 106
long-term memory (LTM), 34–35, 39

marshmallow test, 19–20
mathematics difficulties, 38
meditation, 22

memory. *See* working memory
memory aids, 42
memory games, 63
memory strategies, 107–108
memory traces, 33
memory training activities, 42–43
metacognition, 69
mindfulness, 22, 101–102
mind mapping, 64
mock job interviews, 29
modeling
   appropriate emotional
      expression, 106
   checklists, 109
   classroom organizations, 86
   decision making, 105
   diverse perspectives, 109
   feedback, 106–107
   growth mindset, 107
   long-term goals, 106
   memory strategies, 107–108
   multisensory techniques, 108–109
   pausing before responding, 105
   personal boundaries, 107
   problem solving, 105
   real-life examples, 104–105
   self-monitoring questions, 73
   task breakdown, 108
   think-alouds, 104
movement, 22, 27–28
multiple information modes, 41
multisensory techniques, 108–109
music and movement, 27–28

naming feelings, 22, 22*f*
notebook organization, 85

organizational skills, 10, 72.
   See also planning, organization,
      prioritization, and time management
   thinking, 38

pair reading, 42
parent involvement, 93
pausing before responding, 105
PBIS (positive behavior interventions
   and support) strategies, 92
peer-mentorship programs, 29

personal boundaries, 107
perspective, understanding, 62–63
planners, 85, 86
planning, organization, prioritization, and time management, 4, 13, 79–80, 87
   characteristics of underdeveloped, 83, 84*f*
   organization, 80
   planning, 80
   prioritization, 80
   research findings, 80–82
   SEL connection, 82, 82*f*, 91
   self-assessment, 83, 84*f*
   strategies for older students, 85–86
   strategies for younger students, 84–85
   timeline of development, 81
   time management, 80
plan sheets, 85
positive behavior interventions and support (PBIS) strategies, 92
practice tests, 42
predictability, 10
prefrontal cortex, 15, 35, 89, 102
prioritization. *See* planning, organization, prioritization, and time management
problem-based learning, 63
problem-solving skills, 39, 99–100, 105
procedural memory, 35
processing delays, 38
professional development, 92
project-based learning, 63, 77
puzzles, 99

quality of work, inconsistent, 83

random acts of kindness, 12
reading comprehension, 38
real-life examples, 104–105
reflection activity, 98–99
reflection journals, 28, 65, 76
relationship skills, 11–12
   and cognitive flexibility, 59*f*
   and impulse inhibition, 21*f*
   impulse inhibition and, 90
   and planning, organization, prioritization, and time management, 82*f*
   and self-monitoring, 71*f*
   and working memory, 37*f*
reminders, 41
REM sleep, 35
responsible decision making, 12
   and cognitive flexibility, 59*f*
   and impulse inhibition, 21*f*
   modeling, 105
   and planning, organization, prioritization, and time management, 82*f*
   and self-monitoring, 71*f*
   and working memory, 37*f*
retrieval practice, 41, 42
rhythmic activities, 61–62
rigidity in thinking, 60
risky behaviors, 24
role models, 27
role-play, 97–98
rolling with the punches activity, 28
routines, daily, 26, 59, 65, 100
rubrics, 76

schedule change warnings, 61
school culture, 93
seating arrangements, 62, 74
self-awareness, 8–9
   and cognitive flexibility, 59*f*
   and impulse inhibition, 20–21, 21*f*
   and planning, organization, prioritization, and time management, 82*f*
   and self-monitoring, 71*f*
   and working memory, 37*f*
self-check sheets, 76, 77*f*
self-discipline, 10
self-management, 10
   and cognitive flexibility, 59*f*
   and impulse inhibition, 21*f*
   and planning, organization, prioritization, and time management, 82*f*
   and self-monitoring, 71*f*
   and working memory, 37*f*

self-monitoring, 4, 13, 67–68
　buddy system checklist for, 74, 75f
　characteristics of underdeveloped, 70–72
　defined, 68
　research findings, 69–70
　SEL connection, 70, 71f, 91
　self-assessment, 73f
　self-check sheets, 76, 77f
　strategies for older students, 75–78
　strategies for younger students, 72–75, 75f
　timeline of development, 69–70
self-questioning, 69
self-reflection, 69
self-reflection activities, 65
self-regulation and impulse inhibition, 90
self-talk, 42
SEL skills. *See* social-emotional learning skills
sensory memory, 34
short-term memory (STM), 34
skill transfer, 60
sleep and memory, 35
SMART goals, 86
social awareness, 10–11
　and cognitive flexibility, 59f
　and impulse inhibition, 21f
　and planning, organization, prioritization, and time management, 82f
　and self-monitoring, 71f
　and working memory, 37f
social domain, 8
social-emotional learning
　and EFS development, 94–95
　executive function and, 90–91
　schoolwide SEL, 92–93
　transformative SEL, 89–90
social-emotional learning skills. *See also specific competencies*
　academic domain, 8
　competencies of, 2, 8–15
　domains of, 7–8
　emotional domain, 8

relationship skills, 11–12
responsible decision making, 12
self-awareness, 8–9
self-management, 10
social awareness, 10–11
social domain, 8
social pressure, 11
social skills training, 28
social stories, 62
"social stories," 26
Socratic seminars, 76
Stanford marshmallow test, 19–20
sticky notes strategy, 17–18, 25, 76
story performances, 27
storytelling, 42, 64
stress and memory, 35
stress and self-monitoring, 69
stress response, 10
Stroop test, 58
student choice, 26
student conferences, 77
student emotional expression, 26
subroutines, 41
superhero role-play, 98
survival state, 9
synthesis, 32

tardiness, 83
task breakdown, 108
task initiation, 83
teacher-student relationships, 11–12
team-building, 11
technology integration, 65, 75
think-aloud activities, 42, 85
think-alouds, 104
thinking outside the box activity, 98
think-pair-share activities, 42
This Is Not game, 64
time estimation, 85
time management, 71, 102. *See also* planning, organization, prioritization, and time management
timers, 61, 86
time warnings, 26
traffic lights system, 74
transformative SEL, 89–90
transitions, 38–39, 59, 100

unpredictability, 59

verbal instructions, 41
visual aids, 101
visual checklists, 41
visual cues, 41
visual schedules, 61

working memory, 3, 13, 31–32, 34
    characteristics of underdeveloped, 38–39
    defined, 32
    encoding, 33
    research findings, 33–36
    retrieval, 33
    SEL connection, 37–38, 37*f*, 90
    self-assessment, 40*f*
    strategies for older students, 42–43
    strategies for younger students, 39–42, 39*f*
    timeline of development, 35
Would you rather? activity, 99

yoga, 27

About the Author

 **Marilee Sprenger** is a veteran educator with more than 25 years of experience teaching elementary, middle, and high school. She is an author, a professional development specialist, and a popular presenter at conferences and trainings. She has provided keynote addresses internationally and specializes in social-emotional learning, executive functioning, memory, vocabulary, and the brain.

Sprenger is the author of 18 books on the brain and learning. Her most recent bestselling book is *Social-Emotional Learning and the Brain* (ASCD, 2020). She has written numerous articles and contributed chapters to several publications.

As a member of the American Academy of Neurology, Sprenger stays abreast of the latest brain research and its applications. Her research-based, hands-on approach to professional development leaves educators with dozens of strategies to implement immediately in the classroom.

Sprenger's website is marileesprenger.com. She can be reached by phone at (309) 264-5820, by email at brainlady@gmail.com, and on X (formerly Twitter) @MarileeSprenger.

Related ASCD Resources

At the time of publication, the following resources were available (ASCD stock numbers appear in parentheses).

All Learning Is Social and Emotional: Helping Students Develop Essential Skills for the Classroom and Beyond by Nancy Frey, Douglas Fisher, and Dominique Smith (#119033)

Attack of the Teenage Brain! Understanding and Supporting the Weird and Wonderful Adolescent Learner by John Medina (#118024)

The Brain and Learning (Quick Reference Guide) by Allison Posey (#QRG119045)

Cultivating a Classroom of Calm: How to Promote Student Engagement and Self-Regulation by Meredith McNerney (#124016)

Engage the Brain: How to Design for Learning That Taps into the Power of Emotion by Allison Posey (#119015)

Improve Every Lesson Plan with SEL by Jeffrey Benson (#121057)

Learning That Sticks: A Brain-Based Model for Instructional Design and Delivery by Bryan Goodwin, Tonia Gibson, and Kristin Rouleau (#120032)

Promoting Student Attention: How to Understand, Assess, and Create Conditions for Attention by Robin Wisniewski (#122014)

Research-Based Strategies to Ignite Student Learning: Insights from Neuroscience and the Classroom, Revised and Expanded Edition by Judy Willis and Malana Willis (#120029)

Social-Emotional Learning and the Brain: Strategies to Help Your Students Thrive by Marilee Sprenger (#121010)

Supporting Emotional Regulation in the Classroom (Quick Reference Guide) by Jodi Place (#QRG121062)

Teaching with Poverty and Equity in Mind by Eric Jensen (#120019)

Upgrade Your Teaching: Understanding by Design Meets Neuroscience by Jay McTighe and Judy Willis (#119008)

For up-to-date information about ASCD resources, go to **www.ascd.org**. You can search the complete archives of Educational Leadership at **www.ascd.org/el**. To contact us, send an email to member@ascd.org or call 1-800-933-2723 or 703-578-9600.

The ASCD Whole Child approach is an effort to transition from a focus on narrowly defined academic achievement to one that promotes the long-term development and success of all children. Through this approach, ASCD supports educators, families, community members, and policymakers as they move from a vision about educating the whole child to sustainable, collaborative actions.

The Missing Link to Help Them Think relates to the **engaged, supported,** and **challenged** tenets.
For more about the ASCD Whole Child approach, visit **www.ascd.org/wholechild.**

Become an ASCD member today!
Go to www.ascd.org/joinascd
or call toll-free: 800-933-ASCD (2723)

WHOLE CHILD
TENETS

1. HEALTHY
Each student enters school healthy and learns about and practices a healthy lifestyle.

2. SAFE
Each student learns in an environment that is physically and emotionally safe for students and adults.

3. ENGAGED
Each student is actively engaged in learning and is connected to the school and broader community.

4. SUPPORTED
Each student has access to personalized learning and is supported by qualified, caring adults.

5. CHALLENGED
Each student is challenged academically and prepared for success in college or further study and for employment and participation in a global environment.

DON'T MISS A SINGLE ISSUE OF ASCD'S AWARD-WINNING MAGAZINE.

ascd educational leadership

If you belong to a Professional Learning Community, you may be looking for a way to get your fellow educators' minds around a complex topic. Why not delve into a relevant theme issue of *Educational Leadership*, the journal written by educators for educators?

Subscribe now, or purchase back issues of ASCD's flagship publication at **www.ascd.org/el**. Discounts on bulk purchases are available.

To see more details about these and other popular issues of *Educational Leadership*, visit **www.ascd.org/el/all**.

2800 Shirlington Road
Suite 1001
Arlington, VA 22206 USA

www.ascd.org/learnmore